MW00812635

MURDER & MAYHEM
IN
COLUMBUS
OHIO

MURDER & MAYHEM
IN
COLUMBUS
OHIO

NELLIE KAMPMANN

THE
History
PRESS

Published by The History Press
Charleston, SC
www.historypress.com

First published 2021

ISBN 9781467147316

Library of Congress Control Number: 2021943825

To the victims and their loved ones. May you find peace wherever you are.

CONTENTS

ACKNOWLEDGEMENTS

I would like to thank the following people for their help in creating this book: my film noir buddy Ed Violet for telling me about the Lola Celli case; Fred Alter, who was gracious in allowing me to cover his family's tragedy; the ever-talented Jennifer Roth, who polished my prose; Jessica Jewett, Melanie Samples and Wendy Owen for their advice; Fiverrous, who made some amazing pen and ink drawings for me; my sweet husband, Bob; my editor, John Rodrigue; and all my friends and family who cheered me on.

Trying to write a research-intensive book during all the COVID closures presented some unusual challenges. I am likewise grateful for the online resources that were provided by the Columbus Metropolitan Library, the Grandview Heights Public Library and the Library of Congress.

INTRODUCTION

In the end, we'll all become stories.
—Margaret Atwood

Whenever crimes happen in the modern world, one typically hears a chorus of: "Things like this never happened in 'the good old days.'" Historians know better. If you spend some time looking through Columbus newspapers from the Victorian era or the first half of the twentieth century, you'll find reports of crimes strongly reminiscent of those found in today's world. Like today, some are minor—others are downright bloodcurdling.

A random selection of crimes can be found in a scrapbook in the collections of the Columbus Metropolitan Library. The unidentified scrapbook, which covers the years between 1932 and 1940, appears to have been compiled by either Jacob E. Sandusky, who was the Franklin County sheriff from 1937 to 1947, or someone close to him. The clippings start off with a headline story about sheep rustlers. A couple of others expose the scandals of gambling and immoral dancing at a nightclub. These may sound quaint to modern ears. A clipping about a peaceful sit-down protest at the governor's office that ended in violence from the police echoes more recent events in Columbus's history. Violence against police can be found in others. One set of clippings describes the shooting of a deputy by a teenage girl's mother when he went to investigate a juvenile delinquency case. Some apparently common crimes in the scrapbook might take a modern reader by surprise. Recurring themes of

Postcard of South High Street at night, circa 1910. *Night Scene, South High Street, Columbus, Ohio. Courtesy of the Columbus Metropolitan Library, F.M. Kirby and Company.*

THE OHIO PENITENTIARY.

A 1909 photograph of the Ohio Penitentiary. *Courtesy of Columbus Metropolitan Library.*

hit-and-run homicides and women jumping from or being thrown from cars are found sprinkled throughout the scrapbook. There were also clippings of the more expected crimes, such as bank robberies. A particularly striking newspaper clipping shows convicted bank robber Carl Boettcher being wheeled on a hospital gurney to his new home at the Ohio Penitentiary. Boettcher was gravely wounded in a shootout that killed a police detective. That is covered in the first chapter of this book.

The stories told in this book will feel familiar to the modern reader. There are tales of addicts turning to unlawful activities to support their habits, racially motivated attacks, domestic abuse and gang activity dating back a century or more. Then there are the all-too-common cases of murder for no apparent motivation other than to give the killer a sense of power.

The aftermath of these crimes was often as dramatic as the crimes themselves, the true stories rivaling the most twist-filled fictional detective and criminal trial TV shows. Investigations turned into roller coaster rides of hopes raised, dashed, then raised again. Just when a promising lead looked like it would solve the case, it turned out to be nothing of worth. Key evidence disappeared, and witnesses' testimonies shifted. New, unrelated crimes were discovered as the detectives combed possible crime scenes for clues. Occasionally, the loved ones of murder victims found themselves affected years later in ways that they could not have anticipated. Often, the criminals were caught and duly punished. Other times, there was no retribution.

It seems that when it comes to crime, some things never change.

1
THE GANGSTERS

When people think of criminals from the 1930s, gangsters and bank robbers usually come to mind. The two converged in Columbus on February 4, 1938, resulting in blood and death.

Around 9:30 in the morning, four masked men with .45-caliber guns walked into the Hilltop branch of Ohio National Bank on West Broad Street and started yelling. One jumped the railing and held a gun to the head of assistant manager Elmer J. Hagenberger. Another, who seemed to be the leader, forced manager Curtis G. Wilcox, at gunpoint, to remove money from the vault. The four other employees and four customers were ordered to stand with their hands against the wall by two more gang members. The robbers made off with $3,500, dropping some of the cash in their rush to escape. They fled in a Ford sedan and headed toward Georgesville in the southwest corner of Franklin County.

This was the second time in one week that the area had been hit by bank robbers. The First Federal Savings and Loan bank, right across the street from the Hilltop branch of Ohio National Bank, had been robbed a couple of days earlier. Despite the proximity of these crimes in distance and time, police believed the robberies had been committed by two separate gangs. There was a big contrast in how the gangs operated. The Ohio National robbers were raucous, terrorizing their victims with noisy confusion, while the First Federal robbers operated with quiet efficiency. The license numbers from the getaway cars also did not match.

It did not take long for the police to locate the Ohio National Bank robbers. Several hours after the robbery, authorities received a tip that the gang members were hiding out at a rooming house at 183 Guilford Avenue. Chief of Detectives Harry Carson sent four detectives to follow up on the tip. What started out as a routine check soon turned violent.

Detectives Robert Cooke and Robert R. Cline got out of the car first and knocked on the front door. Since the front room was rented out, Bettie Fisk, the owner, came around the side of the house from the back to speak to them. She verified that men fitting the suspects' descriptions were there. They had rented rooms from her, presenting themselves as students. Their behavior had been suspicious. Fisk mentioned that they had insisted on keeping the doors locked and changing the lock on the garage. They had explained to her that they were worried about their car, claiming that it had been burglarized while it had been parked on the street.

Cooke and Cline signaled to Detectives Leo L. Phillips and William J. Danner to come. As the latter approached, the first two detectives went around to the back of the house. One of the robbers, later identified as "Jake," noticed the police approaching.[1] He opened fire through the front window. At the same time, a flurry of gunfire peppered the back of the house. That volley hit Detective Cline twice in the abdomen. He called out to Cooke to let him know that he had been hit and then crawled to the porch, where he collapsed.

Detective Cooke entered the kitchen and shot Jake through the heart as he came in from the living room. Jake fell down, dead, by the kitchen door. Cooke then saw Violet Wotring, a tenant who had been ironing in the back of the house when the gun fight started. He shoved her under the sink to relative safety. One of the robbers started firing on him from the living room but hit Wotring in the hip instead. Cooke shot the crook in the chest. The man fell back onto the couch in the living room. While Detective Cooke went into the living room, Wotring, whose injury was not serious, grabbed the dead gangster's gun and went out into the backyard.

When Detective Cooke entered the living room, another bandit opened fire on him. He retreated to the backyard, intending to sneak around to the front. There, he saw Wotring holding the gun. He took it from her and used the bullets from it to reload his own revolver. Cooke started heading around the outside of the house when one of the robbers called to him from the kitchen. The gang member, identified as twenty-year-old Stephen Figuli from Cleveland, came out with his hands in the air, giving himself up.

Detective Robert Cline. *Courtesy of Columbus Metropolitan Library.*

Neighbor Lillian McGeary called the police for backup when she saw Detective Phillips gesturing for her to do so. She said that she had heard at least thirty shots fired during the gun battle. In the course of the fight, robber Carl Boettcher jumped through the front window and ran down an alley toward the Pennsylvania Railroad tracks. Detectives Phillips and Danner pursued him. They caught up with him by the tracks at the end of Stevens Avenue. Danner shot Boettcher and disabled him but received a serious gunshot wound to the groin in the process.

Boettcher also managed to shoot Phillips in the corner of his eye. Had the shot been straight instead of at an angle, Phillips would have been killed. As it was, he did not require hospitalization. This was a lucky break for Phillips, who had been off duty the day of the robbery but rushed to the call to pursue the robbers.

Assistant Chief of Detectives Glenn C. Hoffman and Detective George Ruder arrived shortly after the gun battle ended. They found a bloodbath. Detective Cline was near death on the porch. One robber was lying on the sofa, and Jake was on the floor in the kitchen. Assuming that the robbers were both dead, they proceeded to the bedroom. Detective Ruder turned around to see the robber on the couch pick up a large-caliber revolver and aim it at Hoffman. Ruder ran over and kicked the thug in the face, just in time to disarm him before he got off a shot. The villain did not live long enough to make it to the hospital.

Amid sorting out the situation, the police ended up with an unexpected arrest. Wotring's eighteen-year-old son, Fred, who lived in the house with her and a few siblings, was wanted on a warrant for being a fugitive from the Columbus Workhouse. Three other household members were also being held for questioning.

That evening, Detective Cooke was asked to recount the capture of the gang at an annual dinner that launched the Policemen's Pension Fund Board ball campaign. It was a bittersweet retelling, due to the serious injuries received by Cline and Danner. Cline died later that night. Military rites were planned for Detective Cline's funeral the following Tuesday at St. Joseph's Cathedral.

Back at the police station, Stephen Figuli filled the police in on the gang's activities. He identified the dead man on the couch as Vincent Grinkowicz but only knew the other dead man as "Jake" or "Mack."[2] Grinkowicz was listed on his death certificate as a twenty-one-year-old former bakery worker. Their previous holdup had occurred in Cleveland a few weeks earlier. Mack, who led the gang with Grinkowicz, insisted that the gang go to Columbus to rob the bank. He expected that they could get $40,000 from the stickup. They had planned the Hilltop robbery with precision. Jake and Grinkowicz traveled to Columbus several days in advance to set up the robbery, then returned to Cleveland to get Boettcher and Figuli. They holed up in a downtown hotel while Jake and Grinkowicz searched for another place to stay. At one point, Motorcycle Officer Lawrence Tucker followed their car, considering it suspicious.

Figuli's role in the robbery had been to keep the customers lined up against the wall and to help carry out the loot. He confirmed that the gang had not been involved in the First Federal robbery. It was reported that Figuli's share in the Ohio National Bank robbery would have been only $500. *The Columbus Evening Dispatch* sneered at him as being a "sucker" over that.[3] He told the police that he never fired his gun during the ensuing shootout. That contradicted Boettcher's story that Figuli had been the first to fire.

Figuli said that he never intended to shoot a policeman. His only reason for joining the gang was to get back at Vincent Grinkowicz. Figuli elaborated, "I hated him and only joined the gang so that I could get enough money to get him out of the state and kill him. I wanted to fill him full of lead and throw his body in the lake."[4] His anger toward Grinkowicz stemmed from an incident that had occurred several months prior to the bank robbery, when they were in Cleveland. Grinkowicz shot Figuli three times, thinking that he had tipped police off to a bank robbery committed by Grinkowicz's brother. He left Figuli outside of the Cleveland Art Museum, expecting him to die.

Figuli, a self-described "black sheep of the family," started his criminal career in high school.[5] An acquaintance who he knew committed burglaries invited him along one night. From there, he met a safecracker who had been in the Mansfield Reformatory. He was caught after going on a couple of jobs with the guy. That earned him ten months at the Boys Industrial School in Lancaster. There, he met Grinkowicz, who was serving a year for drunk and disorderly behavior. After Figuli got out, Grinkowicz approached him about getting some guns. Figuli joined the gang from there. He had been making his living gambling and hijacking slot machines since June 1936. The young gangster admitted to taking part in a bank robbery in Cleveland on January 14.

Twenty-three-year-old Carl Boettcher was a fellow Cleveland native. He was questioned by Detective Chief Carson in a Mount Carmel Hospital room where Boettcher lay paralyzed from his wounds. Officer Everett L.

Artist's rendering of bank robber
Stephen Figuli. *Author's collection.*

McSaveney called him "a thoroughly tough customer."[6] Unlike Figuli, whom Boettcher referred to as his pal, he was mostly closed-mouthed about his previous criminal career. Upon investigation, it was discovered that Boettcher's life of crime went back to when he was sixteen. He and three of his friends held up a confectionery shop, gaining three dollars. For punishment, he spent time in a California reform school and in a workhouse in Cuyahoga County.

He said that he was sorry for "plugging" Detective Danner.[7] That seemed unlikely in light of other comments he had made. He stated that he hated cops. He blamed them for a "bum rap" he had received several months earlier.[8] Boettcher boasted that the gang had kept guns for the express purpose of shooting cops. According to his statement during questioning, the police had fired first in the shootout. When asked if he would get into a shootout with the police again if he could do things over, he replied, "You're damned right I would."[9] He preferred to die in a gunfight rather than be taken alive.

Boettcher, who had been the driver in the getaway car, bragged that the car he used was a police cruiser. They had stolen it from the Newburgh Heights Police Department near Cleveland. They found the car with the keys in it, so they jumped in and drove away. A shortwave police radio in the car had enabled them to avoid police cruisers. He said that the gang also had a 1937 LaSalle that they had left parked in a lot downtown.

Boettcher shared Figuli's murderous hatred of Grinkowicz. He complained that Grinkowicz had tried to put the blame on him for some bank robberies that Grinkowicz himself had bungled. An unverified report revealed that Grinkowicz's body had at least five bullet wounds and that not all of the shots had come from police guns.

The identity of the fourth man, known to the surviving gang members only as "Jake" or "Mack," proved to be elusive. The police took fingerprints from the body of the unidentified robber to compare them with those kept by the FBI. It turned out that the FBI did not have the fingerprints of the unidentified robber or any of the gang members on file. That quashed the police's original assumption that the unidentified man was Charles

Bird, a notorious bank robber from Cleveland. A death mask was cast from his face and taken to Cleveland for possible identification there. His body was put on display at the Spears Mortuary, where it was viewed by four thousand people. One well-dressed man claimed to recognize him, but he took off before Spears could question him about it.

In Cleveland, James Matzoras identified the man from the death mask as Jacob Miller, who used to cash his WPA paychecks at Matzoras's restaurant. Miller was described as a sandy-haired, blue-eyed man who was six feet, two inches tall and about thirty-eight years old. That description fit the dead bandit. Police had sought Miller a year before the robbery for a series of holdups, but he had no criminal record. Despite that, no conclusive identification was ever made. Per his death certificate, which was issued weeks later, on February 26, he was still officially listed as "unidentified," with only "known as Mack or Jake" noted as possible names.[10]

Chief of Detectives Carson had Detective Cooke prepare charges against the two surviving gang members for first-degree murder. They were pushing for the death penalty. County Prosecutor Ralph J. Bartlett did not want to rush the process, as they did not know whether Detective Danner was going to survive. Happily, Detective Danner was reported as being in a better condition than he had been the previous day. The gunshot missed any vital organs and the abdominal cavity.

Police tried to connect the gang to other crimes in the state, comparing bullets from their guns with others found at other crime scenes. They focused on the murder of Roy "Happy" Marino, a fellow bank robber from Youngstown who was killed in September 1937.

A Franklin County grand jury quickly indicted Boettcher and Figuli on first-degree murder and robbery charges, returning their decision within an hour. The trial date was tentatively set for March 7. Both men pleaded innocent. Boettcher had to do so from his hospital bed, as a bullet that was lodged in his spine made it unsafe for him to be moved. Boettcher declared that he was ready to go to the electric chair.

After a thwarted attempt to change the venue, Stephen Figuli's trial began as scheduled. Kenneth Little and Merle Champ acted as his defense attorneys, with Judge Dana F. Reynolds presiding. Figuli's sister, Julia Hoenick of Cleveland, was in attendance. Twelve jurors were chosen after being questioned about whether they were comfortable with potentially sending a man to the electric chair. They were taken to the site of the shootout. Jurors were shown objects from the house, including a bullet-ridden door and money sacks. A floorplan of the house and crime scene photographs were entered into evidence to further help the jury understand the events of that fateful day.

The expected slew of witnesses, both from the robbery and the shootout, took the stand to give their testimony. A few of Figuli's family members were called in as character witnesses. Some poignant moments came when a tearful Mrs. Cline was asked to identify her husband's clothing. Detective Cooke also gave emotional testimony about finding his friend, Detective Cline, gravely wounded.

A sticking point in the trial was whether Figuli would automatically be up for the death penalty if convicted. That was the sentence based on a recent law that required the death penalty to be enforced for first-degree murder convictions when the murder occurred during a bank robbery. The defense argued that the state could not claim that the death of Detective Cline occurred during the bank robbery, as the shootout occurred six hours later at a different location. They contended that Figuli had not fired the fatal shot and said that the gunfight was not planned.

Figuli told the jury his version of events, reaffirming his claim that he had never fired a gun during the shootout. Figuli stated that he had been asleep when the cops arrived and only woke when Grinkowicz yelled for them to duck as the shooting started. He lay on the floor during the shootout to avoid being hit by gunfire. After the shooting stopped, he considered killing himself. He looked for his gun, which was in his coat pocket. After changing his mind, he tossed the gun somewhere. Assistant Chief of Detectives Hoffmann confirmed this story during questioning. Figuli had told him that he had only one gun in the pocket of his coat in the closet and that he had tossed his gun to one of the other gang members. Detective Cooke noted that one of the shots came from about a foot off the floor.

Figuli swore that the gang had not agreed to have a shootout with the cops if they got cornered. This was contradicted by Assistant Chief of Detectives Hoffmann, who said that Figuli had mentioned that the gang had guns in the house to use against the police if necessary. Judge Reynolds wryly pointed out, "I don't think they had the guns there for target practice."[11]

On March 11, after a little over three hours of deliberation, the jury found Figuli guilty of murder in the first degree without recommendation of mercy. This mandated the death penalty. The next day, Little announced that he would file a motion for a new trial. Despite the undesired outcome, Figuli was fascinated with the proceedings. He was particularly impressed by Prosecutor Daniel Webber's performance during the trial, comparing it to movie-quality acting.

Due to his injuries, Carl Boettcher's trial was pushed back to March 16. The surgery to remove a bullet from his shoulder went well, but he was still in critical condition. He attended his own trial on an ambulance stretcher. He was represented by Attorneys Franklin Rubrecht and Charles Earhart. In lieu of a trial by jury, Boettcher asked to be tried by three judges. The presiding judges were Henry L. Scarlett, Cecil J. Randall and Dana F. Reynolds. Ralph J. Bartlett and Daniel Webber acted as the prosecuting team.

The defense attorneys requested that the judges read the testimony from Stephen Figuli's trial in order to save Boettcher more strain on his beleaguered body. This request was denied, but the witness testimony was given remarkably quickly. Twelve witnesses testified in two hours and fifteen minutes, even with two recesses to attend to Boettcher's medical needs. The trial had an unexpected Hollywood connection. Among the defense's witnesses was his mother, Emily Boettcher, who had been working as a cook for movie star Warner Baxter. She had quit her job in order to be with her only son after he was shot.

The two-day trial ended with Boettcher being found guilty on the count of first-degree murder. Judge Reynolds declared that there were no grounds for mercy, regardless of his fragile physical condition. Boettcher's counsel immediately filed a motion for a retrial.

The following day, Judge Reynolds overruled the motion for a new trial for Figuli. The motivation for the motion was that Fred Delinger, one of the jurors, was the brother of Edward Delinger, who had been in the Hilltop office of Ohio National Bank at the time of the robbery. The brothers had filed affidavits saying that they had not seen each other since January of that year. Judge Reynolds decided that their connection was inconsequential.

Figuli was taken to death row at the Ohio Penitentiary in the custody of Warden James C. Woodard. The twelve condemned prisoners there, along with Boettcher and another man who was expected to be sent there shortly, would bring the number on death row to an all-time high. Figuli was scheduled to die in the electric chair on July 1. Boetcher was scheduled to die on July 29. When the prisoners saw Boettcher being brought into death row on a stretcher, they commented that he was a dead man already. They were not wrong. On April 6, Boettcher died from his injuries at the hospital in the Ohio Penitentiary, his mother by his bedside. His body was immediately shipped to Cleveland for burial.

The next several months yielded a whirlwind of appeals, as Figuli tried desperately not to join his friend in death. He filed an appeal with the

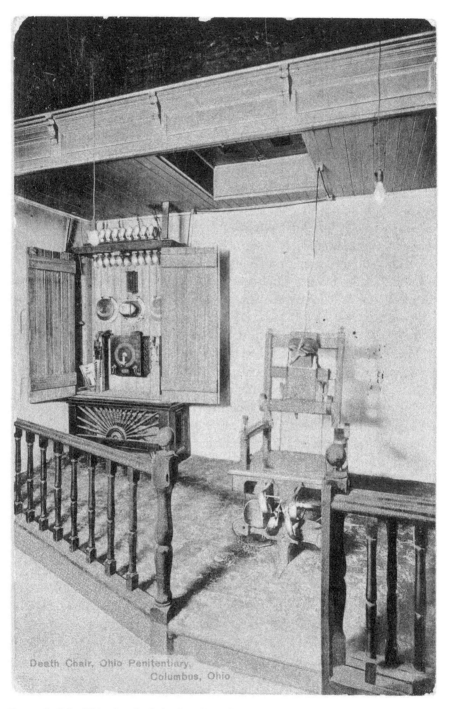

Postcard of the Ohio electric chair, circa 1909. *Death Chamber, Ohio Penitentiary, Columbus, OH;* S.F. Harriman. *Author's collection.*

Franklin County Court of Appeals and was granted a stay of execution. It granted the stay while it decided whether it would permit the defense to file a brief that should have been filed at the time of the appeal. The stay of execution was then extended to September 30 to allow Figuli's attorneys time to complete an appeal to a higher court. Two days before his new execution date, Figuli received another stay of execution, pushing his execution date to October 25.

After considering the appeal, the district court of appeals upheld the county court's decision to have Figuli executed on October 25. It reasoned that although Figuli may not have fired a single shot in the gunfight, he was part of a conspiracy to potentially have a shootout with the police.

Again, with little time to spare, Attorneys Little and Champ filed a notice of appeal to the Ohio Supreme Court on October 22. Figuli was placed under an indefinite stay of execution while the Ohio Supreme Court considered his appeal. Over a month later, the appeal was refused. The new execution date was set for December 21.

With one day to go before the execution, Governor Martin L. Davey refused to intervene on Figuli's behalf. Upon hearing this news, Figuli resigned himself to his fate. He was quoted as saying, "We all have to go sometime. It don't make much difference."[12] Figuli's mother, Susanna Figuli, was not ready to give up. The next day, with the execution scheduled for the evening, she spent her time trying to get a personal audience with Governor Davey to beg him for clemency. Figuli, who had been accepting of his impending death just the day before, began showing signs of distress as the hour of his execution neared.

By the time his appointment with death arrived, Figuli had calmed down again, reiterating that he was not afraid to die. He showed no signs of fear as he walked into the death chamber, a small prayer book in his hand, and sat down in the electric chair. His expression was described as "defiant."[13] His only signs of tension were his clenched fingers as the hood was placed over his face. He was pronounced dead at 8:08 p.m. His mother could not bear to witness his death. She waited in Little's office until it was over. Likewise absent from the execution were the surviving detectives from the shootout.

After Figuli's death, two letters from him were opened. The first was to Governor Davey, which stated that he understood his decision and held no ill will against him. He thanked him for considering his case and wished him the "merriest of Christmases."[14] The other was to an anonymous woman, thanking her for the verses she had frequently sent him while he was imprisoned.

Not wanting the memory of the detectives' bravery and sacrifice to die with the killers, the county prosecutor's office gave a display commemorating the battle to the police. The display, which included guns from the firefight and Detective Cline's picture and badge, was set up in a corridor of the police headquarters.

2
THE BODY IN THE WELL

JANUARY 27, 1889

Truro Township stonemason Walter Collins had a bad feeling. His friend's daughter Sarah Ginever had sent a note to him saying that her father had been missing since Friday night. It was then Sunday morning, and he had a dream the night before in which John Ginever was in a well.

Collins went over to the dairy farm that Ginever owned to look into the matter. There, he found Phillip Sauter, one of the farmhands, in the barn. He asked Sauter where Ginever had gone. Sauter could not say. Collins remarked a couple of times that it was strange Ginever would disappear without word to anyone. The farmhand insisted that Ginever was not far away and would return soon. Collins then asked to see the well in the barn.

Sauter thought that was an odd request. He discounted the possibility that Ginever could be in the well, as they had never used it the entire time he had worked at the farm. The well was in the feed room of the barn, covered up with boards and boxes. When they cleared off the debris and lifted the cover, the water was covered with hay. They forked the hay out but saw nothing to indicate that a body might be down there. Dissuaded from looking further, Collins went up to the farmhouse across the road from the barn to talk to Sarah. He invited her to stay with his family until her father reappeared. It would not have been proper to leave the eighteen-year-old alone with the two young men working there.

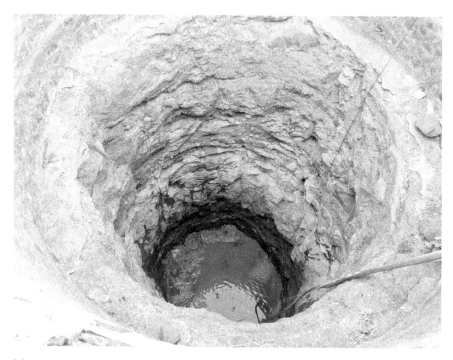

Walter Collins dreamed that the body of his missing friend John Ginever was hidden in a well. © *Kaushal Satpute | Dreamstime.*

A week passed, and Ginever remained missing. Collins could not shake the niggling feeling that his old friend was in the well. He went back to the farm, this time with fellow neighbors Al Seddons, John Vanderburg, Thomas Ash and one other man to examine the well more closely. The corner of the barn was dark, so they had Sauter bring a lantern to them. They had to rake off a layer of straw from the top of the water. Once cleared, they sent down a grappling iron. That brought up a basket and a bucket from the well. On the second try, they retrieved a piece of cloth. Then the hook caught what they had both hoped for and feared—it was a leg.

In their excitement, they knocked the lantern out. They yelled to Sauter for help. Sauter claimed that he was too busy putting the cattle out to help them. When they asked him for a rope to bail the water out, he said that they had none. The men found some rope at the tool house. Once they had Ginever's body removed from the well, they brought it from the dark feed room of the barn to view it in the light. They found that Ginever's pockets had been turned out as if he had been robbed. The cap he had been wearing before he disappeared was missing.

The police uncovered more clues as they scoured the farm for the next few days. They brought a lantern into the feed room to better inspect the crime scene. The feedbox, walls and ceiling were splashed with blood. It had seeped into the ground. A hatchet, spade and sack in the room were also bloodstained. Ginever had been hit so hard that a bit of brain matter had been flung from the blow. From this gory evidence, the officers determined that Ginever had been killed while standing at the feedbox, mixing feed for his cattle.

They noted that the well was in a spot where one would not think to look. It was covered with boards, a box and hay. When they removed everything from the top of the well, there was more hay covering the water. They decided to bail the foul-smelling water out to search for more evidence. The stench was so bad that they had to take turns. When Engineer Brodie finally descended a ladder to the bottom of the well, he could only stay for short periods, as the foul air made him ill. Aside from a large stone, there was only some small detritus that added nothing to the investigation. They considered that since the stone was on top of the other things, it may have some bearing on the case. A search of the other outbuilding did not come up with anything useful.

A disturbing story came out in the witness interviews. Ginever's wife, Hannah, had died three years earlier under mysterious circumstances. The official story was that she died after her dress caught fire. She lingered for a few days before succumbing to her wounds. The neighbors who were caring for her were shocked when, in her final hours, she kept repeating, "Oh, why did you set me on fire?"[15] They suspected that she was referring to her husband. Since there was no firm evidence to back this up, the matter was dropped.

Suspicions soon fell on one of the two farmhands living at the Ginever farm. Phillip Sauter was a twenty-four-year-old man from Stuttgart, Germany. He had worked for Ginever previously but had left to work at another farm for a year and a half. The calm, heavyset young man had been back working at the Ginever farm for a couple of months. Sarah described Sauter as being like a member of their family. She had gone with him to an opera house once with her father's permission. She scoffed at the idea of them being romantically involved. As the daughter of his employer, she felt herself above being courted by the hired help. Regardless of their relative positions in life, she did think highly of Sauter. She said that his relationship with her father was pretty good but admitted that Ginever had once whipped Sauter so badly that there was blood on the curtains.

Sauter's view of his relationship with the Ginevers was different from Sarah's perception of it. He had written a letter to one of his brothers in Dayton saying that he liked the girl very much but did not like her father. That was followed with a request for advice as to whether he should marry an English girl or a German one. Sarah had lived in England as a child. Sauter's attitude toward Ginever changed a bit when he spoke to the police. He told them that Ginever had treated him with kindness.

The other farmhand, Gustavus "Gus" Benz, had only been working for the family for a few days at the time of Ginever's disappearance.[16] Sarah was less impressed with him, indicating that he drank too much and was unreliable. She claimed that they had only hired him out of a sense of charity.

Sarah Ginever recounted the night of her father's disappearance. Her father came back from town in the evening in a good mood. Then something set him off, and he struck her so hard that she fell down. She told Sauter about the incident. Other witnesses had mentioned that Ginever frequently struck his daughter—much to the anger of Sauter. One man said that one time she had been whipped so hard that she slept all night in the outhouse. That man added that Sauter and Ginever had been in a fight. Sarah continued, saying that Ginever and the farmhands were sitting around chatting until about 9:00 p.m., with Sauter being mostly silent. He and Ginever then went out to the barn, telling Benz that his help was not necessary. Sarah stayed in the house with Benz and read *The Mystery of a Hansom Cab* to him.[17] Sauter came back around 9:15 p.m., commenting that Ginever was still out in the barn. The farmhand went into a workroom. After a few minutes of washing his hands and some milk cans, Sauter came out and went to his room for the night. The dogs started barking, so Sarah looked out toward the barn. She noted that a light was still on in the stable. Unconcerned about the dogs, she continued reading. Later on, Benz left to go into the city.

Police found $64.35 and a bloody handkerchief among Sauter's belongings. The blood on the handkerchief was determined to have come from a nosebleed. Just outside his room, they found a pair of pants with one leg curiously cut off just above the knee. Before the police investigation had begun, Sarah found Sauter's oilcloth apron in his room. It appeared to be freshly washed but had been stained. Police took it as evidence.

Sauter appeared untroubled when he was placed under arrest the same day the body was discovered. Later that evening, the police took him to the morgue to see if they could rattle him into a confession. Sauter again affirmed that Ginever was too kind to him for him to ever have wanted to kill him.

A couple of weeks later, Phillips Sauter was arraigned before Mayor Philip H. Bruck. Attorney Cyrus Huling led the prosecution, and D.T. Ramsey acted as the defense attorney.

Police Superintendent John E. Murphy gave a grisly testimony about the physical evidence of the assumed crime scene. Spots of blood on the feedbox, located about fifteen feet away from the well on the ceiling of the barn, led him to believe that the murder had taken place there. Ginever had blood and feed on his hands. Murphy surmised that Ginever was killed while mixing feed for the horses. The bucket and basket used for mixing were found in the well. He pointed out that they were used daily and would have been missed if they had been in there before the day of the murder.

A bloody hatchet found by Murphy became the center of conflicting testimonies. Sauter claimed that he had brought it into the barn to cut some boards, but there was no evidence that he had cut any. Earlier on the morning of Ginever's disappearance, Ginever asked where the new hatchet was. Sauter, who was apparently absent when Ginever was looking for it, told the others that it was in the barn. When Ginever inquired about it again in the evening, Sauter told him that he didn't know. According to Sarah Ginever, her father was rather protective of his new hatchet. He never allowed anyone but himself to use it and never used it in the barn. She introduced new information: shortly after her father went to the barn on the night of his death, Sauter came in the house saying that Ginever had sent him to fetch his hatchet. Then, on the Tuesday after the disappearance, Sarah told Sauter to bring the hatchet back to the house. He did not do so, saying that he was using it in the barn. That did not make sense to her, as her father had an old axe in the barn for the farmhands to use. She said that her father got angry when things weren't done the way he wanted.

Dr. Josiah Medbery performed the autopsy under the direction of Coroner Patrick A. Egan. He explained how the damage done to Ginever's scalp and skull indicated that the weapon used was a blunt instrument. The back of his brain had a wound an inch and a half in diameter, which was consistent with the blunt end of the hatchet found at the murder site. The right side of the brain was pulpy.

Detective Patrick Kelly testified that Sauter had told him that the blood on the hatchet had come from killing a chicken. A professor of chemistry at Starling Medical College, Curtis C. Howard, was given manure, the hatchet, items of men's clothing and a red handkerchief for testing. In his professional opinion, the blood that was found in the manure and on the hatchet was not that of a farm animal.

The money found in Sauter's possession was another matter of concern. Detective Kelly said that while Sauter claimed he had saved $50.00 from his earnings, he was found to have $64.35. Sarah Ginever avowed that shortly before the murder, her father had given Sauter $9.00. After the disappearance, Sauter paid $5.00 for an order. She noticed, at the time, he had a handful of silver.

Sauter's trial began on July 2. Judge David F. Pugh, irritated by a tardy witness, announced that he intended for the trial to be concluded by the end of the week.

Sauter stared impassively as the jury was selected. The prosecution made sure that the jury members were willing to convict on circumstantial evidence, knowing that would mean Sauter's execution.

Prosecutor Huling painted Ginever as a difficult man who was so hard to please that his daughter was afraid of him. She sat up all night waiting for him when he disappeared because she didn't know whether he would be angrier if she had locked the door or if she hadn't. She thought that he had just gone into town that night. When Huling recounted how the fatal blow must have been struck, she became so distraught that she had to leave the courtroom.

Defense attorney M.B. Earnhart attested that the night before Ginever was killed, soldiers had been in the barn. One of them had lost a badge there, and it indicated they were from Company A. Earnhart observed that Sauter had been asleep in his bed at the time of the murder but that the family dogs had been restless and noisy.

Augustus Albert Benz, the other farmhand, gave testimony that he had been hired to work on the farm just a few days before the murder. He gave an account of the day's activity. Ginever left around 7:00 a.m. and did not return until 3:00 p.m. Meanwhile, Benz and Sauter had been baling hay all day. On his return, Ginever called Sauter down from the hay loft, where the farmhands had been working, to have him unhitch the horses. When Sauter came back, he told Benz that Ginever had slapped his daughter. Sauter added, "If Ginever comes up here and picks a fuss with me, you go out and leave us alone."[18] The Ginevers and the farmhands had supper together around 7:00 p.m. Afterward, Sauter left to work in the barn. Ginever followed him a half hour later. Benz never saw Ginever again. After Sauter went to his room, Benz heard snoring coming from there shortly after 9:00 p.m. Benz then went to a quieter part of the house.

Benz followed this testimony with an account of the Sunday evening after the murder. He returned to the farm about 7:00 p.m. to find Sauter sitting in the kitchen, smoking. Sauter told him that Sarah had gone into town and had all the interior doors locked up. Sauter said that they could sleep in Ginever's room that night. Sauter removed the lock on the door with a screwdriver. He also broke open doors that led into the hallway and one at the top of the stairs.

The star witness, Sarah Ginever, covered most of the testimony that she had given in the arraignment, but gave some additional information. The idea that Sauter had killed Ginever to protect Sarah was reinforced by her description of the Saturday night after the murder. She and Sauter stayed up all night to wait for her father. They sat on opposite sides of the stove— Sarah in a chair and Sauter reclined on the ground with his back against a chair. Sarah noticed that he had a revolver on the floor next to him. She ordered him to put it away, as there was no need for it. She noted that he never used it around the house but would take it with him when he went into town. Since she had already stayed up the previous night, she drifted in and out of sleep. Whenever she woke up, she noticed that Sauter was watching her. She did not recall him saying anything about the soldiers being in the barn on Thursday.

Neighbor Martin Dibble did back up the defense's story about the soldiers. According to Dibble, Ginever had told him that he had shot at some soldiers. Playing up the possibility that soldiers had killed Ginever, the defense again pointed out the strange behavior by the dogs after Sauter had come back into the house the night of the murder. Sarah reported that the dogs were running along the road, barking and carrying on. She clarified that while the dogs were running back and forth between the house and hedges along the road, she was sure that happened a couple of days after her father disappeared.

Earnhart had Sarah's previous testimony read back by the court stenographer. She had originally said that Sauter was gone for fifteen minutes. In her redirection testimony, she admitted that she was busy with housework and did not know how long he had been gone. That raised the question as to whether he could have been gone long enough to kill Ginever and hide his body. John Vandeburg and Frank Sauter, who had been at Walter Collins's house after Phillip Sauter's arrest, gave the same account that Sarah had given them earlier. As they recalled it, she had said that the accused had only been at the barn with her father for a few minutes.

Two receipts for malt that Sauter had in his possession were brought in for examination. They were from two different days the week before the murder. A cashier for the Hoster Brewing Company testified that Ginever rarely settled his accounts with them in person. He remembered giving the receipts in question to someone other than Ginever, but he could not remember who. If Ginever never had the receipts, Sauter could not have robbed Ginever of them while allegedly picking his pockets after the murder.

The finances of both Ginever and Sauter were delved into, with close attention paid to both of them. The prosecution declared that Ginever had $100.00 on him when he came home the day of his murder. C.W. Hedge stated that Ginever was in his barbershop the day of his disappearance and had a bag of money on him. Sarah Ginever mentioned that Sauter had asked her father for some money the day before the murder so that he could go to the theater. Her father gave him $5.00. Her father carried money—part of which was silver—in his hip pocket. According to George Dun, the secretary of the police board, Sauter had a roll of bills, some coins and a watch and chain on him when he was arrested. The cash totaled $65.37. The defense argued that the money Sauter had was saved by him while working at another farm before being employed by Ginever. Farmer Louis Gieger, Sauter's previous employer, confirmed that he paid Sauter well enough for him to have saved that amount in the year and nine months he was employed by him. He started Sauter off at $10.00 a month, eventually raising his wage to $14.00 a month. He had also given him $30.00 the month before he left.

The defense called witnesses to counter the claims that no one but Ginever was allowed to use the new hatchet and that it was never used in the barn. Asa Lindsey, who worked for Ginever the week after Sauter was hired, said that he used the hatchet to chop corn. He admitted that he did this without Ginever's knowledge or permission. Fellow farmhand Simon Huffman claimed that he was the first of the farmhands to use Ginever's new hatchet. He testified that after Sauter had come to work there, it was used just as often in the barn as it was at the house. He recounted an incident in which Ginever was concerned Sauter was mishandling the hatchet by using the blunt end as a hammer on a barn repair. Ginever relaxed when Sauter promised to buy him a new hatchet if he broke it.

Another point of contention in the trial was whether the well was truly as much of a secret as the prosecution made it out to be. Simon Hullman testified that he had seen the well uncovered before the search for Ginever's body.

Finally, Sauter, whom several witnesses had described as "a quiet, peaceable, industrious man," was put on the stand.[19] He spoke of his background—being born in Germany to a family of seven siblings, four of whom had immigrated to America. His mother had passed away, but his father was still alive. When he first came to America, he worked in a couple of places in New Jersey before coming to Columbus to help his brother with stonecutting. He met Ginever one winter while he was out in the country east of Columbus. Ginever offered him a job at five dollars a month, then raised that to ten dollars a month in the spring. His workday was from 4:00 a.m. to 3:00 p.m. Sauter took care of the farm while Ginever was out making milk deliveries.

He told the jury of the night Ginever struck him. Ginever had come home around midnight after a night of drinking. Sauter tended the horses. He let Ginever know that he was worried about one of the horses, as it seemed sick and was not eating. Once inside, Ginever went upstairs and ordered his daughter out of the house. She stayed away for the rest of the night. After she left, he beat Sauter. The next morning, Ginever blamed the assault on his having been drunk. In her earlier testimony, Sarah Ginever had corroborated that her father may have been drinking that night. Ginever treated Sauter's black eye with some medicine. Sauter claimed that had he had no hard feelings toward Ginever over that incident. He did continue working for Ginever for a while.

He eventually quit the Ginever dairy to go work for Geiger. He left Geiger's farm after working there for a year and a half. When he ran into Ginever at a saloon, Ginever offered him ten dollars a month to come back and promised to repay some of the money that was owed him. Sauter said that he had over seventy-two dollars saved when he returned to work for Ginever.

Sauter denied Dibble's claim that he threatened to kill Ginever if he ever hit Sarah again. He said that their conversation consisted of Dibble complaining that Ginever was difficult to get along with.

On the night of the murder, he went to the barn to feed the cows after supper and moved some hay to the other barn. Ginever asked if he was done for the night. He replied that he was going in in a few minutes. Ginever went to feed the horses while Sauter took another ten minutes to finish up his work. The farmhand went to the coal shed to get some coal for the house. He set the coal beside the stove, washed some pans and went to bed. He denied having anything to do with Ginever's death.

When asked why Benz left his job at the farm, Sauter admitted that Sarah was unhappy with his drinking. She checked with Sauter to see if he could handle all of the work. When he said yes, she let Benz go.

Sauter accounted for him and Benz breaking into Ginever's room to sleep there a couple of nights after their employer disappeared. Sauter and his coworker rationalized this on the basis that Ginever's room was warm and

A typical late Victorian Ohio farmhouse that was similar to the Ginever home. *Photographer, Ben Shahn; courtesy of the Library of Congress, Prints and Photographs Division, Farm Security Administration/Office of War Information Black-and-White Negatives.*

had a nice bed—there was no point in letting that go to waste. The same went for some cider from the cellar that Benz procured.

Sauter explained that the revolver he kept beside him the night that he and Sarah stayed up waiting for her father was not in working order. He had gotten in the habit of carrying it, as they had had some problems with theft around the farm. Thieves had boldly entered the house's cellar and stolen some cider that very week.

During cross-examination by the prosecution, he was asked if he had borrowed five dollars from Joseph Kessler when Kessler asked him to attend a dance. At that point, Sauter turned pale, his eyes rolled and he passed out. He was revived. Police Surgeon Schulze examined him and proclaimed that he was just suffering from exhaustion. The court went into a recess, and then the questioning resumed. Sauter answered that he had only asked to borrow one dollar, as he had no change, but Kessler gave him five dollars.

After eight and a half hours of deliberation and eight votes, the court declared a hung jury. Judge Pugh set bail at $4,000, with the expectation that Sauter's brother in Dayton, who owned a farm, would cover it. His brother, who had already paid for the defense, was unable to bail him out.

Another five months went by before Huling had Sauter retried for murder. The trial started on December 4, 1889. While it was largely a rehash of the previous trial, some new things came to light.

In the intervening months, Sarah Ginever had married Ed Haag and moved back to her father's farm. Her husband found a lantern in the barn that she identified as the one Sauter used. It had spots on it that she believed to be blood. Professor C.C. Howard, who had testified in the previous trial, ascertained that the spots were too old to test accurately. The defense reminded her that when Sauter's brother had come to pick up his possessions, she had given him a lantern that she said belonged to the accused. Sarah insisted that the lantern then in evidence was actually Sauter's.

J.K. Hunt testified that just before the murder, he went to the Ginever farm to collect some money that Ginever owed him. Ginever said that he did not have the money. This strengthened the claim that the money found on Sauter was not stolen from Ginever's dead body.

Former neighbor Sarah A. Innis recalled a conversation she had with Ginever the night that he struck Sauter. Ginever came to her house after the incident, thinking that his daughter might have retreated there. He filled her in on the situation, saying he was very sorry that he had hit the young man. Ginever's story was that he was sleeping off a bout of drinking when he heard Sarah's voice coming from Sauter's room. He was so angry at the impropriety of his daughter being in a man's bedroom that he intended to kill both of them. Instead of finding anything scandalous, when he entered the room, he found Sauter mending some clothes. Still riled up over what he had expected to see, Ginever struck him, hard.

Witnesses were brought in to testify about the problems that Ginever had been having with soldiers from a nearby garrison. They were a known problem in the area, frequently coming to the local farms to help themselves to what they could find. Frank Greile said that he saw Ginever on horseback, chasing down a soldier. When Ginever caught the man, he forced him to give back some apples that he had stolen. The prosecution pointed out that for apples to have been ripe, that would have had to have occurred several months before the murder.

David Horocker recounted a more troubling story. While he was at Ginever's house the Sunday before the murder, Ginever had told him that his life was in danger from the soldiers. Ginever feared that he was "liable at any time to have his head knocked off" by them.[20] He assured his friend that he was ready for them.

After thirteen hours and thirty-five minutes of deliberation and several rounds of voting, the trial ended with another hung jury. Prosecutor Huling announced that he intended to try Sauter a third time.

On July 3, 1890, after Sauter had languished in jail for seventeen months, Huling decided not to put Sauter on trial for a third time. He conceded that the jury was split even further at the second trial than the first. This made it unlikely that the result would be any different at a third trial.

The aftermath of the murder brought both tragedy and triumph to the two key players in the trial. Sarah Ginever Haag inherited her family's propensity for miserable endings. She died in 1926 of dysentery in the Lima State Hospital. In contrast, Phillip Sauter's life took an upward swing in the years following his release. He became naturalized in 1892 and married in 1901. After working as a stonecutter and laborer, he found his calling as a fireman. When he died in 1926, his tombstone in Mount Calvary Cemetery was inscribed, "Died a Happy Death."

3

THE CHRISTMAS EVE COP KILLER

The holidays are supposed to be a time of warmth and celebration. Strangers merrily wish each other well, friends raise a glass in cheer at parties and families indulge in a deeper sense of togetherness. Sadly, for many, the holiday season only serves to ratchet up tensions that have been simmering all year. This was probably on Jessie Mann's mind when she went to the police station late in the afternoon on Christmas Eve in 1908 to report that her brother was abusing their mother—again.

The home at 103 West Rich Street had long been filled with strife. The root of the problem was a difficult relationship between Harry Hillyard and his married sister. He believed that Jessie looked down on their family in favor of the family she had married into. Their father had bankrolled Jessie's husband, Howard O. Mann, to allow him to open a store. Since their father's death, Harry had been supporting his mother. He felt that it entitled him to tell his mother who she could and could not have in their home—that included Jessie. Any time his sister came to visit, there was a row. When she stopped by to wish their mother a merry Christmas, he flew into a rage, targeting his mother for disobeying his orders.

This was nothing unusual. Hillyard was already well known to the police for his drunken furies. His mother had filed numerous complaints against him for mistreating her when he went on drinking sprees. Even as a boy, he had been prone to trouble. He had spent time at the Boys' Industrial School in Lancaster for delinquency. Wanting to get away from his domestic conflicts, he had recently started to move some of his belongings out of

Artist's rendering of Officer
Harry Campbell. *Author's collection.*

the house to set up housekeeping with a young woman. The promise of peace on that front was short-lived. When the police informed him that he would still have to support his mother and treat her properly, he abandoned that plan.

On the day in question, Patrolman Harry Ellis Campbell was interrupted from his other duties at police headquarters and sent off to handle the Hillyard situation. Indiana-born Campbell had spent most of his life in Richwood, Ohio, where his parents still lived. An avid outdoorsman, he honed his shooting ability while serving in the cavalry in the Spanish-American War. After the war, he worked in the offices of the Big Four Railroad in Columbus and then joined the Columbus Police in July 1905. That suited him well. He quickly worked his way up from the lowest ranks. His office skills came in handy for the job. For the month or so before the Hillyard situation, he had been assigned to special duty to assist Secretary Tom Guthrie in compiling the annual report.

Desk duty temporarily set aside, he headed off for the Rich Street address. Domestic violence calls were always a bit dodgy. Often, the abused became protective of their abusers and begged the police not to arrest them. Other times, the people involved were furious at having the police interfere in what they felt was a family matter. It wasn't unusual for the violence to be turned on the attending officer by both the abuser and their victim. This call turned out to be far worse.

At 4:45 p.m., just as Patrolman Campbell started up the front steps of the Hillyard house, Harry Hillyard shot him. The twelve-gauge blast from the single-barrel shotgun tore through Campbell's badge and chest just above his heart. Campbell fell to the ground, unconscious. A patrol wagon soon arrived to find the drunken Hillyard standing beside the wounded officer. Patrolman Campbell was loaded onto the wagon to be rushed to nearby St. Francis Hospital. Before they could make it there, the wagon was rerouted to the morgue. Campbell had died, leaving behind a wife and five-year-old son.

Hillyard unabashedly took credit for the killing, saying that "no one else was to blame."[21] He was led off to jail by Detective John W. Davis, aided by Engineer Lewis, Chief Deputy Police Clerk Malloy and Operator John

Park. Later, in his cell, he said that when he saw the officer on his doorstep, he had a crazed desire to shoot. Witnesses suggested that there was a bit more premeditation than that. When his sister took off to get help from the police, they heard him threaten to kill the first policeman who came across the street. Once Hillyard shot Campbell, his first impulse was to run away. He quickly decided against that and chose to take what was coming to him.

The day after Christmas, Harry Campbell's body was brought back to his home after being prepared for burial. He was moved, escorted by an honor guard, to lie in state at Memorial Hall, where his funeral was to be held. Every available police officer was expected to be at the funeral in full dress uniform to show their respect for their fallen comrade. The next day, he was buried at Green Lawn Cemetery. There was a sizeable turnout from the community. This was not just out of general sympathy for his death in the line of duty; in addition to his involvement with the United Spanish War Veterans, he had been involved with ten other organizations, including several hunting and fishing clubs, Woodmen of the World and a telegraphers' association.

Sitting in jail over Christmas gave Hillyard time to think. The gravity of his situation began to sink in. No longer was he the unrepentant man he had been at the time of his arrest. He was slouched and indifferent. He was also alone. He received no visits from friends or family, although his mother forgave him enough to send over a basket of food for his lunch.

Hillyard was arraigned on January 16, 1909. In defiance of his undeniable culpability in the homicide, he pleaded not guilty to the charge of first-degree murder. It was assumed that his defense would be argued on the basis of emotional insanity, lacking premeditation or malice. Whatever his defense was, he was found guilty of a lesser charge at his trial in April. Instead of receiving a death sentence, Hillyard was sentenced to life in prison. Even that lighter sentence was lifted after a decade and a half. On September 21, 1923, Harry Hillyard was released from prison.

4
THE LEGACIES OF MURDER

On March 31, 1948, police were called in to investigate two stabbing murders. Both were of women. The cases were soon found to be unrelated, yet years later, they both affected the victims' families in unexpected ways.

The first murder occurred at the Ohio Hotel, close to Union Station on North High Street. Policemen David Siegle and Pat Morgan were called to a second-floor room, where they found the body of a scantily clad mystery woman. She had been beaten on the head with a wine bottle and stabbed about twenty times with a penknife. An apple was shoved into her mouth, adding a chilling edge to an already horrific scene.

Three hours later, in the nearby East Side, the body of middle-aged housewife named Marcella Smilack was discovered by her husband in their basement when he came home from work. Police determined that she had been stabbed with a butcher knife while standing at the sink in the kitchen, getting ready to wash dishes. Her body was then dragged downstairs. The lone piece of evidence was a small brown button that had gotten tangled in her hair.

Overwhelmed with two murders at once, Captain Glenn C. Hoffman, chief of Columbus detectives, quickly assigned six additional detectives to handle the cases. That tripled the number the department normally had. They were broken into two squads, one for each murder. Sergeant Edgar "Sparky" Reeves, who oversaw the police identification and scientific crime detection bureau, said that they had taken an unprecedented number of photographs for the two cases.[22]

At first, it looked like the cases might be related. They soon realized that this probably was not the situation. The two victims and murder scenes were as different as they could be.

The hotel victim was the kind of exotic person you might expect to see in a film noir movie. She was a youngish Jane Doe with dyed red hair and five tattoos on various parts of her body. Her "work worn" hands led police to suspect that she had been a war worker.[23] They hoped to identify her either through her tattoos or fingerprints, which were potentially on file in Washington, D.C. The many empty wine and beer bottles found in the waste basket in her room suggested that she was a bit of a partier.

Marcella Smilack was more of a "salt of the earth" type. A housewife in her early sixties, she had four grown children and was married to scrap metal dealer, Herman Smilack. She had emigrated from Russia forty years earlier. Smilack filled her spare time by being active in the Agudath Achim Congregation, the Agudath Achim Sisterhood, the Hadassah and the Ladies Mizracht.

The nameless "bad girl" quickly captured the imagination of the press as her story became more lurid. According to C.L. Brown, the owner-manager of the Ohio Hotel, the victim had checked into the hotel the previous afternoon with a man, who registered them under the fictitious names of Mr. and Mrs. G. Carr of 1783 Zanesville. They left the hotel later that evening, only to come back intoxicated a while later. Hotel employee Delbert Foster saw the man again when he came back downstairs shortly after midnight. "Mr. Carr" hung out by the pinball machine to smoke a cigarette, then walked out. The man crossed High Street and hailed a southbound cab. Brown, Foster and Close all described him as a five-foot-nine man around forty to forty-five years of age and 165 pounds in a two-toned brown-and-tan checked sports jacket, gray pants and a brown hat. The next afternoon, Brown found the body of the woman in bed with a blanket thrown over it. Despite the violence of her death, the other guests had not heard any suspicious noises.

Police began to make progress in identifying the victim. Two waitresses from a grill near Lincoln and High Streets recognized her as being a woman who had frequented the establishment in a WAC uniform. They told police that she had dated a man who was then in the Columbus Workhouse as a prisoner. That man recalled having a date with a woman who fit the description of the five-foot-seven, 135-pound victim. He only knew her as "Phyllis." The detectives got another lead when a taxi driver reported picking up a woman fitting her description along with a male companion.

The woman passenger had complained of having a back tooth extracted. They followed up with area dentists.

The Smilack case was likewise yielding promising leads to follow up on. A few weeks earlier, two seventeen-year-olds had stolen the car of Marcella Smilack's son Dr. Benjamin J. Smilack. They were brought in for questioning. The boys had no reason to seek revenge against the Smilacks, as Dr. Smilack had not pressed charges. The detectives also were looking at two handymen who worked in the neighborhood as possible suspects.

The neighbors turned out to be a good source of information. According to them, Marcella had been working in the yard earlier in the day. She typically left both the kitchen door and the one leading outside to the basement open in good weather. Mrs. H.O. South, who lived nearby, reported that her children saw a man entering Marcella's home two hours before her death. When Sue, Nancy and Robert South came home for lunch, they saw a man go from the front part of the Smilack house to the back. He unlatched the gate, went up on the porch and entered without knocking. The intruder was about five feet, ten inches tall and 170 pounds, and he was wearing blue trousers, a tan leather jacket, a brown felt hat and brown shoes. Police disclosed that they were holding a tannish topcoat in connection with the case. While it was not a jacket, like the young witnesses had described, the coat had what looked suspiciously like bloodstains on it.

The next few days brought in more information on the Jane Doe case. The medical report provided the grim clarification that the woman had already been beaten to death with a wine bottle before she was stabbed twenty times with a small knife. Witnesses mentioned that the victim had a large purse and a camel hair coat when she had registered at the hotel. Neither of those had been found in her room. The police did find the taxi driver who had picked up her companion after he left the hotel. The driver told them that the man had him drive southbound on North High Street. After going only a short distance, the man ordered him to pull over and let him out.

A woman who viewed her body at University Hospital recognized the victim as having frequented bars and taverns near Broad Street and Central Avenue. Other leads indicated that the victim had traveled with a circus or carnival.

The Jane Doe was finally identified by her fingerprints at the London Prison Farm and the FBI. She turned out to be Mona McBride, legally known as Etta Marian Ferguson. McBride was a former café hostess and "carnival queen."[24] New Orleans police had sent her fingerprints to Ohio in 1937, when she was a fugitive from the law. They provided the information

Mona McBride worked in carnivals, such as this one, circa 1930, before moving to Columbus. *Glenelg Sideshow Area Showing People; courtesy of the History Trust of South Australia.*

that she was a café hostess who had previously lived in Denver and Salt Lake City. According to the FBI, she had been arrested for vagrancy in Fairfield, California, under the name Mary Anderson. Their records listed her as having been born to L. Brown and Catherine Bowman on July 15, 1918, in Yuma, Arizona.

A new witness supplied yet another alias for the deceased. A man from Alger, Ohio, claimed that he had given her a ride to Columbus on February 1, 1948. That time, she called herself Marion Carr. She mentioned that she was a waitress in Columbus, living with her uncle John Martin on either North Fourth Street or East Fourth Avenue. No one by the name of John Martin was listed in the city directory on either street.

Squad Two was having better luck in finding suspects for the Smilack case. The detectives brought in a Benton Avenue man as their "best lead" in her murder.[25] He had been arrested on a tip and was found to be carrying a large pocketknife. They followed up with the man who was seen by three neighbor children. He had been seen begging on the streets near the victim's home. A junk dealer who had been in the neighborhood on the day of Smilack's murder had also been seen knocking on her door. Unfortunately, none of the leads panned out. When the police gave an update to her family a week after the murder, all three suspects had been cleared and released.

The following week presented the first suspect in the McBride case. He was a man who was being held for an investigation of grand larceny. The suspect had given McBride a ride from Pensacola, Florida, where he found her hitchhiking on December 13. They went to Tampa, then came up to Columbus. He dropped her off near Fourth and Main Streets, then went to his own home in Richmond, Ohio. He told the police about several other men she had been with. That lead withered away when witnesses from the Ohio Hotel were not able to identify him as the man she had registered with.

Mr. and Mrs. L.B. Bowman arrived from Portland, Oregon, and identified McBride as their daughter, Etta. They related more of Etta's tumultuous life to the detectives. She had left home when she was seventeen, following the separation between her and her husband, Harvey Dell Ferguson, when their infant son, Larry, was only eight weeks old. She left her baby behind in the care of her parents. Their last contact from her was a letter dated December 23, 1947, which was postmarked in Columbus. She wrote that she was working at the Grand Café at 312 South Fifth Street and that she was "alive and well."[26] The Bowmans only found out about her death when an uncle in Denver, Colorado, read about the case in a newspaper. It was a devastating blow for them and their four surviving daughters. The Bowmans had already lost their only son, Benjamin, in a traffic accident just two weeks before Etta's murder.

Things were heating up for Squad One. Five men and two women were then being held at the city prison in connection with the McBride slaying. Most of the detainees were under investigation for burglaries and grand larcenies. Another suspect was an employee of the hotel. All of the suspects either knew or had contact with McBride. One of the men claimed he knew who murdered her. He admitted to being with her but not on the night of her death. As the best suspect in the case, he was questioned by the detectives for a grueling one hundred hours.

More suspects came into consideration. The police arrested a young truck driver in connection with her murder. They looked at a Marion Road butcher who was twice McBride's age and who said that he had stayed with her at a Parsons Avenue hotel. This time, she used the name Mary Burge. Police did not consider the butcher to be a serious suspect. A better suspect was arrested shortly thereafter in a downtown hotel. The Zanesville man was under suspicion due to some bloodstained clothing that had been left at an East Side cleaning establishment.

Attention soon focused on McBride's missing purse and camel hair coat. The detectives developed a new theory that the killer had entered the room through a fire escape. They based that on the knowledge that "Mr. Carr" had left without her purse or coat. Earlier in the investigation, they had received a telephone tip on the whereabouts of McBride's coat. They found the bloodstained coat in the North Side address that the caller had directed them to. The detectives arrested a forty-four-year-old Kleiner Avenue woman as the probable tipster.

The Smilack case was not going as well. The one suspect they had in the case was not a strong one. Sergeant John Curtis admitted that they were "practically without a clue."[27] When four sweeping raids brought in dozens of men suspected of pickpocketing, burglary and theft, Squad Two questioned thirty of them in connection with the Smilack murder. Smilack's family tried to push the case along by offering a $500 reward for information on her murder. They directed informants to their lawyer, Goldie K. Mayer.

On the third week of the investigations, suspects continued to pour in for the McBride case. Police questioned two men who had been seen in her company. They absolved a former liquor inspector of any involvement in the murder but still held him on forgery charges in another case.

A more promising suspect appeared in the form of a Detroit nightclub emcee who was arrested in Toledo. He had worked as a nightclub master of ceremonies at a North Side nightclub. Suspicions were raised when he left town the day after McBride was killed. Witnesses tentatively identified the emcee as the man who had registered at the hotel with McBride. The detectives went back to Toledo to check on his story. Another Toledo connection came in the form of two female acquaintances of McBride who were from that city. One was a housewife, and the other was a nightclub employee. They had come to Columbus to establish an alibi for the nightclub emcee.

After May 4, when the detectives questioned an eighty-year-old ex-convict from the Ohio Penitentiary about McBride's death, both cases went cold.

The McBride investigation went back into high gear on July 16. Three uniformed policemen, who had been conducting an investigation on their own, homed in on a "knife-wielding Filipino woman."[28] The woman was a suspect early on in the investigation but had been released by the detectives. The uniformed officers based their suspicions on several points:

1. The woman blamed McBride for her imprisonment in the city workhouse.
2. She threatened to "carve up" a certain woman when she got out of the workhouse.[29]
3. She was registered at the Ohio Hotel at the time of the murder.
4. The officers believed that the nature of the killing indicated that it had been done by a woman.
5. The suspect had served time for "cutting to kill."[30]

The Columbus Evening Dispatch noted that, while McBride had been slashed repeatedly, her death was caused by strangulation. This was in conflict with their earlier reports that said she had been beaten to death.[31]

Detectives tracked the suspect down to her home in southern Ohio, where they found her to be a married woman with a newborn. Upon questioning, it was determined that she was a friend of another woman who was originally thought to be Mona McBride. Police knew of the other woman. This lead had been given by two men who said they had dated the Filipino woman and Mona McBride. It turned out to be a case of mistaken identity. Detectives once again cleared her of suspicion.

On January 15, 1949, there was a new development in the Smilack investigation. Eighteen-year-old John Britton of 261 South Twentieth Street confessed to the murder. Like the latest suspect in the McBride case, he had already been questioned early on in the investigation. Back then, he had told the police that the murder had been committed by two members of the "East End Gang."[32]

This time, Britton had been brought in for attempted auto theft. He and two friends had gotten a ride from Arthur Williams of Grove City and then attempted to steal his car. Williams grabbed the car keys and yelled for help. The three car thieves were tracked down by their footprints in the snow. While Britton was being taken to the county jail from a hearing in Grove City, he asked Night Marshal Kermit Kellar what the minimum age was for execution in the electric chair. The marshal suspected that he was referring to the Smilack case. He told Britton that any information he had about it was important. Britton confessed to breaking into the house using a "gimmick," thinking that no one was home.[33] When Smilack entered the kitchen, she screamed in alarm. Britton said that he panicked, grabbed a knife off the table and started stabbing her.

Detective Sergeant Lowell Sheets was called in to question him. At first, Britton refused to talk further. During a second round of questioning, some inconsistencies arose in his story that didn't fit the crime scene.

The death certificate of Etta Ferguson, also known as Mona McBride. *Courtesy of the Ohio History Connection.*

Sheets began to doubt his confession. Another issue was that Britton did not fit the description of the man who was seen at the house by three neighbor children.

The afternoon after Britton confessed to the murder, he retracted it. He admitted that he had heard about the murder through an East End Gang member named Curley. He said that he confessed to cover up for members of the gang. Detective Chief Glenn C. Hoffman decided that Britton had not known enough of the particulars of the case to be a viable suspect. Britton's parents pointed out that he could not have done it, as he had been stationed at Fort Bragg in North Carolina on the day of the murder. The detectives contacted the army to verify that. The army confirmed that Britton was at Fort Bragg on the day of the murder. Britton admitted that he didn't know if the elusive Curley, whom police had not been able to track down, had actually done the killing. He explained that Curley seemed like the kind of person who would, as he was always playing with knives.

A month later, on February 20, the McBride case blew wide open when another woman was found stabbed to death in the Waldo Hotel, next door to the Ohio Hotel, where McBride had been killed. The murder was eerily similar to that of McBride. The victim was Esther Seibert, who, at twenty-eight, was almost the same age as McBride. Like McBride, Seibert had a police record, frequented area bars and grills and went by an alias, Esther Mason. A man checked himself and Seibert into the hotel, registering them as Mr. and Mrs. A. Warren. There was evidence of drinking in both cases. James Mullins, the room clerk and night manager, described the man as being forty-five years old; five feet, six inches tall; and about 150 pounds with dark, bushy hair. This was not far off from the description of the man who checked in with Mona McBride. Police arranged to have the handwriting in the register compared to that of McBride's companion.

Seibert was discovered by Bellhop Coleman T. Merchant when he went to wake up another guest on the sixth floor. He saw Seibert's door open and a man running down the hall. After glancing in the room and seeing bloodstains, he gave chase down a fire escape. He caught up with the culprit in a parking lot at North Pearl and East Chestnut Streets, where the man threatened him. Merchant backed off and called the police.

A *Columbus Evening Dispatch* reporter noticed that the pieces of blanket inside Seibert's coat looked like blankets used at the city prison. Helen Hank, a workhouse matron, matched the cloth to the blankets. She tentatively identified the victim as a woman who was frequently arrested for drunkenness. Seibert was positively identified by her sister Irene Hoffman of 591 Franklin Avenue. Hoffman said that they had come from Kentucky and that their parents were dead. She confirmed that Seibert used the name Mason as an alias and was an alcoholic despite her family's efforts to "straighten her out."[34]

A couple of days later, Claude Ramsey, a thirty-nine-year-old ex-convict and truck driver's assistant, was held for questioning in the slaying of Esther Seibert. Ramsey had previously been convicted on a charge of strong-armed robbery. He served time for that at the Ohio State Reformatory in Mansfield. He was paroled but had been reported as a parole violator a couple of months before McBride was murdered.

An East Main Street bartender said that Seibert had been at his bar on Friday night with a man who had identified himself as Claude Reynolds.

The Davidson (later Waldo) and Ohio Hotels, where two similar murders occurred a year apart. *Courtesy of Columbus Metropolitan Library.*

Police tracked him to the home of his mother and stepfather, Mr. and Mrs. A.M. Warren, whom he lived with. The police had just talked with the Warrens the day before during a routine check. Ramsey said that he had been barhopping and ended up at the East Main Street bar where he met Siebert. They left with three bottles of beer and took a cab to the vicinity of the Waldo Hotel. Ramsey said that he remembered registering at the hotel, going to the room and removing his coat shirt and shoes. Then, the next morning, he remembered putting his coat on and leaving via the fire escape. He also recalled someone yelling at him and throwing away the three bottles of beer that he had carried out with him. Ramsey wandered around the west side of the Scioto until daylight. He went to the federal building across Marconi Boulevard from police headquarters and asked a guard about seeing someone regarding his income tax return. The guard told him that the building was closed. Unable to complete his errand, he spent the day and night watching movies at downtown theaters. He took a bus to West Town Street to spend the night with a friend. On Sunday, he went back to the movies before returning home. He went to work the next day at a furniture store where he was a driver's helper, only to be told that he was fired for being a no-show on Saturday. He wandered around for the rest of the day, returning home at 5:30 p.m.

Ramsey admitted to fleeing the hotel after being in the room with the victim and throwing away his cap and knife as he ran. When questioned about the murder, he said that he had lost his head and his "mind went blank."[35] He conceded, "I probably did it. She got mad at me, and I got mad at her."[36] When the official charges were brought against him, he pleaded innocent.

The next day, police connected Ramsay with the January 20 death of Mabel Lucille Meadows at the Southern Hotel. Police Chief Frank M. Harrison asked hotel staff throughout the city to cooperate with the police in their efforts to prevent sex crimes. He instructed that the hotels should immediately report suspicious people who register with them. The police compared the Southern Hotel register to those of the Ohio and Waldo Hotels to determine if the same man signed all three at the time of the murders.

The concerns about sex crimes were not warranted in Meadows's death. Her cause of death was recorded as respiratory failure related to pneumonia. Ramsay acknowledged going to the hotel with Meadows after they had met in a downtown grill and later attended a movie together. He claimed that he left the hotel after only fifteen minutes because Meadows had a bad coughing spell. According to Ramsey, she had been fully clothed and sitting in a chair when he left. Her body was discovered nude and covered by a blanket eighteen hours later.

A handwriting expert determined that Ramsay's signature in the Waldo Hotel registration book did not match that of the man who signed himself and McBride into the Ohio Hotel. While he was apparently not the bogus "Mr. Carr," the detectives continued to investigate him in connection with that case.

In March, Squad One shifted its attention to another suspect. This time, it was a twenty-five-year-old navy veteran. The suspect, who was originally from around Athens, had lived in Dayton for several years. He was in Columbus when McBride was murdered and fit the description of the man who was in a taxi with her that night. Police were frustrated when doctors at the Dayton Veterans Hospital would not allow them to question him. Detectives took the matter to the Montgomery County Probate Court. Judge Rodney Love ordered the suspect to be held for mental tests.

There was another lag in the McBride investigation until September 26, when Squad One was contacted by authorities in Ogden, Utah, regarding Ray Dempsey Gardner, a prisoner from Columbus who was in their custody. Gardner was bound for trial for the murders of Shirly Jean Gretzinger, a sixteen-year-old babysitter in Utah, and Sue Horn, a ranch cook in Montana. Gardner confessed to those murders and to the murder of James Shelly, his previous cellmate, at Jamestown, North Dakota. He had been questioned in connection with several other western and midwestern murders. The Columbus detectives said that they would show his photograph to witnesses but did not think that there was strong evidence to link him to the case. They were correct. Gardner was cleared of the McBride murder when it was found that he had been in a western penitentiary that day.

The McBride case took a strange twist on June 30, 1950. On that day, Robert Segee, a twenty-one-year-old who was indicted on two counts of setting minor fires in Circleville, confessed to the Ringling Bros. Circus fire in 1944 and four murders. The circus fire killed 168 people in Hartford, Connecticut. In confessing to his crimes, he made crayon drawings of them. An additional drawing looked remarkably like the hotel room where McBride had been killed. Police questioned him in connection with the McBride murder, but nothing came of it.

One last suspect made the news in the McBride case in August 1953. A Greensboro, North Carolina man, James Roy Johnson, confessed to the strangulation and stabbing murder of his wife, Bessie, in a hotel room in 1951. He made the confession to a tavern waitress in Columbus at the Franklin Café on East Town Street. Johnston said that he always felt like he was being watched and had her call the cops on him. Johnson was a former cab driver whose Greensboro police record showed that he had lived in Columbus in 1948. Police decided to question him about the McBride murder. Much to their disappointment, there was no connection.

While the murders of the women remained unsolved, their impact was felt for years.

On May 21, 1952, Smilack's son Oscar Smilack, a civil rights worker and operator of the Randolph Iron and Metal Company, was indicted by the Un-American Activities Commission for refusing to answer questions about his alleged financing of the Communist Party. In a letter to the editor after Oscar's death in 1968, his friend Genevieve Wilson asserted that he was never a communist but had been targeted by the committee due to his civil rights activities. Oscar's refusal to testify was a misdemeanor punishable only by a fine per the Ohio General Code. He paid far more dearly than that. The man who fought for the civil rights of others soon found his own rights violated.

Prosecutor Ralph J. Bartlett painted Oscar Smilack as an unwitting aid to the Communist Party. He claimed that Smilack suffered from severe psychological trauma after his mother's murder and urged Judge John R. King to send him to Lima State Hospital for thirty days. Smilack was committed without the proper legal procedure of a formal hearing as to his mental condition or evidence given to prove his supposed insanity. Oscar Smilack's attorney, American Civil Liberties Union lawyer Jack Dworkin, filed an application for habeus corpus with the third district court of appeals. The application stated that the indictment was "fatally defective."[37] The defect was that it did not charge a crime for which a conviction could be obtained, even if all the facts set forth in it were true.[38] The court agreed, but its decision was appealed. In 1953, the Ohio Supreme Court upheld the third district court of appeals' decision, noting, "The sending of a person to an institution for the criminal insane, even for a short time, is a serious matter, and his confinement there is as full and effective a deprivation of personal liberty as is his confinement in jail."[39]

The following year, Larry Bowman, the son McBride had abandoned as a baby, likewise had his life changed by her death. Being raised by his grandparents, whom he called "the best people on earth," did not free Larry from the wayward tendencies he had inherited from his mother.[40] He developed the same restlessness that had troubled her. In 1950, at the age of fifteen, he left his home in Yucaipa, California, to join the army. He was discharged less than a year later for lying about his age. He was a drifter after that, falling into alcohol and drug abuse, often living on the streets and begging desperately for food. After a few years of that rough lifestyle, he got it into his head that he needed to go to Columbus to search out his mother's grave in Union Cemetery. He stole a car in Los Angeles in order to get here. Inevitably, he got caught.

Federal judge Mell G. Underwood was going to put him on probation for the car theft. Bowman, much to everyone's surprise, asked to be placed in federal prison instead. He said that he wanted to take his punishment. Bowman explained that the arrest was a wake-up call for him. He was afraid that he would revert back to his old ways if he did not force himself to straighten out. He told the judge that he intended to spend his time in prison studying religion. Judge Underwood was taken aback by the request but complied, sentencing Bowman to eighteen months in prison.

While justice worked in strange ways for their sons, the two murdered women ultimately had none. The leads in both cases were eventually exhausted. The investigations stalled out. Aside from an occasional mention in "unsolved crimes" human interest stories in the newspapers over the years, the murders became forgotten by all but Smilack's and McBride's loved ones—and their murderers.

5

THE CHINESE QUESTION

The northeast corner of Broad and High Streets in downtown Columbus is exactly what one would expect of a busy corner in a bustling city. The flashy electronic advertisements and running news banners look like the futuristic vision of a city in the old science-fiction movie *Blade Runner*. In 1982, when *Blade Runner* came out, people visiting this corner of downtown would have been greeted by the neon waterfall sign for Roy's Jewelers. Going back another century, they would have seen something quite different: a Chinese laundry owned by one of the more curious characters in Columbus history.

Won Koon, who later changed his name to Ben Hope Lee, came to the United States in 1867. He first shows up in the Columbus City Directory in 1876 as the owner of a laundry. Lee was a savvy businessman who understood the value of promotion. His frequent advertisements in *The Columbus Evening Dispatch* soon paid off. By the following year, his business had become so successful that he was able to move it to the prominent corner of Broad and High Streets. Eventually, the business expanded to two locations, adding tea and East Asian novelties to its offerings.

This was a difficult era in which to be Chinese in the United States. The Chinese first started coming to the United States en masse in the early 1800s. They came to seek out better opportunities and, later, escape civil war in their home country. While some of them were merchants or sailors, many worked as unskilled laborers either on the First Transcontinental Railroad or in agriculture. Between Americans' inherent racism and fears

This editorial cartoon points out the prejudice against Chinese people during the Victorian era. *Courtesy of the Library of Congress.*

that the Chinese were taking jobs from them, they soon became targets of discrimination. They were beset by violence and legislation aimed at restricting their rights.

Despite his status as a successful businessman, Lee was not immune to the harassment. One day, a boy threw a dead rat into Lee's establishment and ran off. Lee gave chase. He caught the boy, intending to force him to take the rat carcass away. Instead, a large brute of man took hold of Lee. The man started to drag him to a more secluded place to give him a beating. Luckily, a police officer showed up just in time and led Lee's would-be assailant away.

Given the general attitude toward the Chinese, Lee was surprisingly well respected within the Columbus community as a whole. When former president Ulysses S. Grant visited Columbus in 1879, Lee was included in the reception committee. Newspapers across the state lauded him in their coverage of his marriage to Laura Clarey, the daughter of local mechanic James Clarey, in June 1881. Instead of the expected cries of miscegenation, his wedding was treated like a high-society event. The wedding at Western Chapel Methodist Church on Town Street was fairly large, with one hundred guests. It was followed by a sumptuous Chinese feast for fifty of the attendees. The newspapers fussed over the diamond cluster ring Lee presented to his new bride and the diamond necklace and gold bracelets presented to her by his friend Jow Hong. They marveled at his wealth, which was more than the average person would make in several lifetimes. The reporters were fascinated by the exotic Chinese delicacies served at the dinner and the exquisite Chinese vases used to decorate the room. When the newlyweds went back to China to visit Lee's family a few months later, *The Columbus Evening Dispatch* mentioned the trip in a society column that also mentioned the Prince of Wales's activities.[41] The Lees left on their journey a week after Laura's sister Belle married another Chinese laundry owner, Yew Wing.

Wedded bliss did not last long for the Clarey sisters and their Chinese husbands. Laura and Belle both filed divorce petitions on May 20, 1884. The newspaper article that announced the petitions was slavering at the prospect of juicy gossip coming out in the divorce cases.[42] Divorce was scandalous enough back then without the couples involved being so wealthy and "exotic." To the gossipmongers' dismay, the Lees apparently patched things up. After the initial announcement, no more was said about the divorce in the newspapers. Laura was still shown as being married to Ben Hope Lee in the 1900 census.

Trouble reared its ugly head again two years later, when Lee's cousin Ong Q. Chung died in mysterious circumstances. Chung had recently immigrated from China and bought a laundry at 62 East Spring Street. Edward Green, who owned the saloon next door, became concerned when a tall man passing by the saloon harassed Mrs. Green around 11:00 p.m. Green shooed him off, but he stuck around nearby, acting suspiciously. They suspected that he was a prowler. Green sent someone to get the police. By the time they arrived, the man had walked into Chung's laundry. The business had closed for the night hours ago. The police found the possible prowler sitting in a front office. When they went into the back room, they saw a partially undressed White man sitting in a chair near a bed where Chung lay. The man claimed that he had just stopped in to pick up his laundry. Police ordered him and the other man to leave.

Chung, who spoke little English, pantomimed being strangled. The police left, hoping to catch up with his assailants. Chung then went out to sit on his front stoop. About an hour later, a customer came into the saloon and reported that Chung had fallen asleep on the pavement. Green went to check on him. The laundryman was barely breathing. He died soon after the police arrived a second time. Lee identified him at the morgue. Surprisingly, the police surgeon Dr. Evans said that he found no evidence of violence. Chung's dilated eyes indicated that he had not been poisoned. The final analysis was that Chung had died of heart disease.

A White woman who worked at Chung's laundry related a disturbing story the next day to a reporter who was investigating the case. A tall, drunken man had come into the laundry in the early afternoon, flashing a large sum of money. He began cursing all Chinese and asked her how she could work for such "despicable" people.[43] He boasted that he had just killed one Chinese person and would kill them all. The laundry worker said that Chung had made some enemies recently when he accused several men of stealing his gold watch.

The following decade was a quieter one for Lee—at least in terms of how often he was mentioned in the papers. It was still a busy period. He expanded his laundry business to Mount Vernon. He moved there as well but continued to keep an eye on his Columbus business interests.

His next mention in the newspapers turned out to be an unsavory one. On November 28, 1898, *The Columbus Evening Dispatch* reported that twenty-one Chinese men had been escorted by police out of an opium den owned by Lee on Third Street. The next day in the courtroom turned out to be a bit of a circus. The police were not sure that the men in court were the same ones who had been taken from the opium den the day before. Many of them were found to be out-of-towners. Adding to the confusion were a couple of

An 1884 advertisement for Ben Hope Lee's business interests. *Courtesy of the Columbus Metropolitan Library.*

extra Chinese men who had been brought into the mix. One was Long Hi Sing, a chubby, cheerful man who had come from Philadelphia to act as an interpreter. Another was an unusually burly man who had not been seen the day before; he turned out to be Long F. Chung from New York. He was a "peace distributer" for the Highbinders, an organization that was likened to a Chinese Mason group.[44] His job was to smooth things over when the local organizations got into trouble. He also acted as an interpreter.

The trials began swiftly but chaotically. Swearing in was unfamiliar to the defendants. Lee had to demonstrate it to a few of them in the hallway before court was brought into session. One man had procured a chicken, thinking it would be needed to swear in in the Chinese style. Long Hi Sing acted as the interpreter for the defense. Another man from Dayton, Song Hop, handled the interpretation for prosecution. Throughout that trial, the two quarreled over whether one or the other was giving an unbiased interpretation. The exasperated judge finally yelled at them to shut up. This backfired. The two interpreters suddenly "forgot" how to speak English and kept up their argument in Chinese.

Lee turned out to be the only witness in his defense. His story was that the gathering was a meeting of the Nie Hing Society, a branch of the San Francisco–based Six Companies. The Six Companies was a benevolent association devoted to helping the Chinese population in the United States, acting as a social safety net and fighting against anti-Chinese racism. The court was not convinced. Lee was found guilty of operating an opium den.

Meanwhile, Sam Hong, a businessman from Dayton, filed a petition against Lee in common pleas court. He originally claimed that $600 had been stolen from him while he was getting doped up in the establishment. By the time he filed the petition, he changed his claim to say that he had lost $1,000 at an undisclosed location while playing fan tan, a game of chance, with Lee.

Several days after Lee was found guilty of the opium den charge, a motion was filed to grant him a new trial. Judge Swartz, who presided over that hearing, was aggravated when it was determined that the Highbinders were not a Chinese branch of Masonry. He asked for an investigation into the threats against Sam Hong and his nephew Seung Hop, who instigated the police raid on the opium den. The incident occurred when the two men were leaving the police station to return to their hotel. A gang of Highbinders headed toward them. As one of the Highbinders rapidly approached them, Lee ran interference. He stopped the man before any harm was done. Seung Hop told the police that he had heard the Highbinders threatening to shoot him and his uncle. The two were then put under the protective custody of Court Bailiff Richard Owens. Neither Lee nor Hong could identify the man who had stormed toward Hong.

Defense Attorney Del Saviers cast suspicion back on Sam Hong and Seung Hop, suggesting that they trumped up the allegations for their own benefit. He alleged that they had started the prosecution as part of a conspiracy to blackmail Lee for $1,000. The danger to the two men also appeared to be exaggerated. A rumor had been circulating that a letter had been sent from Chicago offering a reward to anyone who killed Sam Hong and Seung Hop. Police could find nothing to substantiate that. Detective Humble testified that when the police raided Lee's establishment, they found the Chinese men setting up a table for a banquet. That fit with Lee's testimony.

After three of the men who had been arrested for visiting the alleged opium den had been acquitted, the court dropped the charges against the other twenty-one men. Lee did not fare as well. Judge Swartz denied the motion to give him a new trial. He was fined twenty-five dollars and court costs. Saviers asked for a fifteen-day suspension of his sentence. Lee's second attorney, a Mr. Koons from Mount Vernon, asked for leniency, reminding the judge of Lee's otherwise sterling reputation. He promised to take Lee back to Mount Vernon and keep him away from Columbus if the judge suspended his sentence.

While Lee was in a city prison awaiting Judge Swartz's decision, it came out that he had an opium addiction. He was allowed sparing access to

Ben Hope Lee's laundry on the northeast corner of Broad and High Streets. *Courtesy of the Columbus Metropolitan Library.*

opium to avoid withdrawal symptoms. Lee was finally released after paying the fines.

The police were eventually vindicated in their pursuit of opium dens in Columbus. On June 24, 1900, they raided 166 North Third Street, which was owned by Lee Yang. They knew that an annual meeting of Chinese society was scheduled to be held soon. They waited until out-of-town Chinese people showed up in the city and began making their way to Lee Yang's establishment. Once the raid sprang into action, they were not disappointed. They came upon a fan tan game in progress. Behind the game area was the smoking area, which was littered with opium pipes and their users in various rooms. The main smoking room was filled with berths for the customers to lounge in as they smoked. The raid yielded nineteen arrests.

Ben Hope Lee was not involved this time. After his release from prison two years earlier, he had returned to Mount Vernon to live out the rest of his life in relative peace.

6

THE OTHER ONE-ARMED MAN

It should have been a lovely evening on April 25, 1951, for Russell Alter and his family. After a long day at his job as a railroad fireman, he was looking forward to showing his stepfather and mother, Mr. and Mrs. Aytch C. Druggan, the Alters' new home. The Alters had bought it three months earlier. He would also get to spend time relaxing with his wife, Ruth, and cuddling their seventeen-day-old son, Clarence Frederick.

Instead, they found horror.

When they got to the house, Russell told his folks to go in while he went to check the mailbox. They could hear little Clarence Frederick wailing. There was nothing unusual about that—all babies cry. What was odd was that the front door was unlocked. As someone who had previously spent sixteen years as a special deputy and had run his own security agency, Russell was cautious about keeping the front and back doors locked, even when the family was home. An outer door that was normally shut was held open with a block.

The sense Russell had that something was wrong was proven true. His mother directed him to Ruth, who was lying face-down in a pool of dried blood on the kitchen floor. She was still clad in the red chenille robe Russell had seen her in that morning. Blood was splattered around the living room and bedroom. Even Clarence Fredrick's crib was marked with it.

Alter immediately assumed that Ruth had had a hemorrhage. He called to his mother to get the baby while he went to call the sheriff and their family doctor. He also called his ex-wife, Betty Leaman, to see if she could

Artist's rendering of the Alter home. *Author's collection.*

take care of the baby. He had been divorced from Leaman for two years, but he and Ruth were close friends with Betty and her new husband, Robert.

After Dr. David arrived, he examined Ruth and delivered horrifying news. She had not had a hemorrhage—she had been murdered.

A cadre of law enforcement officers soon arrived on the scene. Once the deputies started their grisly work, Alter could not keep his composure any longer. He sat down on the front steps of his house and broke down into sobs, asking, "Why, oh why?"[45]

There was a lot to sort out at the crime scene. Ruth appeared to have been beaten to death. Bloodied newspapers and chamois cloths were found under her body. There were a couple of pearl buttons scattered on the floor that looked like they had come from a woman's garment. They did not match any buttons found in Ruth's wardrobe or button box. Blood-soaked pillows and a broken lamp in the bedroom led investigators to believe that the attack began there. The deputies had found six rifles and shotguns as well as two revolvers in the home. Given Alter's previous work in law enforcement, that was not alarming.

A few days later, Alter reported that a wristwatch, a cigarette lighter and seven dollars were missing. That led police to consider burglary as a motive for the killing. Family members believed that some of Ruth's large jewelry collection was also missing.

Ruth's body was taken to the Ohio State University Hospital's morgue for examination. Dr. Emmerick Von Haam, the pathologist in charge of autopsies there, discovered strands of hair clutched in her hands. The strands were silky, six-inch-long hairs that were light brown with sections of gray at the ends. They were consistent with the hair of a woman. It was later revealed that the strands of hair had been unintentionally washed down a drain by a hospital attendant.

County Coroner Dr. Robert Evans listed a broken neck as Ruth's cause of death, with beating as a contributing factor. She had been severely beaten on her forehead, face and the top of her head. He posited a connection between the heelless loafer found at the scene of the crime and her injuries. He thought the nails that had been exposed on the sole of the shoe after the heel had been ripped off may have caused the puncture wounds found on Ruth's head. According to his findings, there was no evidence of molestation. The time of death was determined to be sometime in the morning, although it had originally been reported to the press as 6:00 a.m., give or take an hour.

Meanwhile, the police interviewed a bevy of witnesses. Most of the neighbors saw or heard nothing of note. Those who had heard something had similar stories. The Alters' backyard neighbor, Mrs. Luther Matthews, told them that a salesman wearing a blue-gray suit had been seen in the area around 8:00 a.m. Mrs. Daniel Russell said that a man knocked on her door at 8:45 a.m. but left before she opened it. She saw a late-model blue Chevrolet parked across the street from the Alter home at that time. Later, she saw him enter the vestibule of the Alter house. The salesman at her door was described as a "well-built" man between five feet, ten and five feet, eleven inches tall and about 180 pounds. Mrs. Ruth Ward described seeing the same man and car. E.A. Rosenbloom, whose house was diagonally across the street from the Alters' house, also had someone knock at their door at 7:45 a.m., only to leave before he could answer it.

Clyde McMurray, a funeral escort service operator, was able to help narrow down the time of death. He called the Alter house between 8:30 and 8:45 a.m. to see if Russell Alter was available to work that day. Alter had previously been a sheriff's special deputy for sixteen years and still worked as a funeral escort on the side. Alter was on call at his main job, which made his schedule unpredictable. When McMurray called, Ruth informed him that her husband had already left for his railroad job. McMurray definitively identified the voice on the phone as Ruth's. He had spoken to her many times and was familiar with her voice. He described

Ruth as sounding calm that morning. McMurray remembered the time of the call because a certain children's program that his kids regularly listened to was playing on the radio while he was talking to her.

Police tried to piece together a better idea of what Ruth was like. At thirty-two, Ruth Alter was not the typical new bride and mother of that era. Originally from Roseville, Ohio, she had worked a "Rosie the Riveter" job at the Curtiss-Wright plant in Columbus during World War II. After the war, she went to work at the Broad-Hague Restaurant as a waitress. It was there that the dainty, one-hundred-pound woman caught the eye of Alter, who was a regular customer. Her delicate build and quiet voice belied her self-assured, efficient personality. Clyde McMurray said that Alter described his wife as not "beautiful, but she's a wonderful girl."[46]

Next-door neighbor Glen Post gave some insight into the Alters' relationship. The Alters had invited him over the night before Ruth's murder to watch television. He described the Alters as being affectionate with each other. He had never heard them quarreling in the three months that they had lived there. Post said that on the morning of the murder, he saw Russell Alter leave the house and drive off about 5:30 a.m. Post stayed home for a while after that but did not hear any noises from the Alter house.

The discarded strands of hair soon became a point of contention. The matter was brought up by prosecutor Ralph J. Bartlett in another case against William R. Russell for the beating death of William S. Grabow. He used it to question Dr. Von Haam's competence. Bartlett implied that Von Haam had carelessly lost the hairs while performing Ruth's autopsy. Von Haam replied, "They were lost because the coroner refused to accept them as evidence."[47] Von Haam clarified that he personally considered them to be evidence but that it was the coroner's decision to make. In his testimony the following day, Dr. Evans claimed that the hairs had already been lost before he arrived at the hospital.

Questions were raised as to whether Sheriff Paul was equipped to handle the case as expertly as was needed. The concern was over a lack of appropriate manpower. The previous month, Sheriff Paul had asked the county commissioners for an additional $55,000 to improve the services his department could provide. They turned him down due to lack of funds. The sheriff's crime lab facilities only included a photographic department and the ability to take fingerprints. Fred Dengert, chief investigator at the London Prison Farm, offered his staff and a mobile crime lab to help with investigations.

Two days after Ruth's murder, the police found their first suspect. The man, a twenty-six-year-old railroad worker from Marion, had been arrested in Richland while wearing bloodstained overalls. They quickly ruled him out as the murderer. He did not fit the description of the man seen on the Alters' vestibule, and he did not have any scratches on his face. Due to substances found under Ruth's fingernails, investigators thought she had scratched her killer.

By the following day, they had questioned six other suspects and were looking to have them take lie detector tests. They believed that the killer was someone Ruth knew.

Russell Alter was among the suspects. Since spousal murders are common, it is standard procedure to consider the victim's spouse a suspect until they are cleared. He was brought in for questioning and to take a lie detector test. The questioning shed more light on the multiple firearms found in the Alter home. It was discovered that Alter had recently sold his private agency, the West Side Merchant Police. He passed the lie detector test and had a verified alibi for the time of the murder. A deputy described him as coming through the examination "as clean as a hound's tooth."[48] After a couple of days in police custody, Alter was released from the county jail and cleared of suspicion.

Alter announced that he would conduct his own investigation with the police. He had already formulated some ideas about the case. He doubted that the killer was a woman, believing that it would have attracted more attention if a woman had come to their home than a man. He also speculated that if the murder had been planned, the killer would have done it at night, when Alter was often at work.

Progress continued to be made as the days passed. A salesman told the police that he had been to the Alter home between 10:15 and 11:30 a.m., but no one answered the door when he knocked. Police Detective Madeline Baker was assigned to track down the origin of the two pearl buttons that were found by Ruth's body. Police took pictures of the crime scene and had the county engineer's staff take precise measurements of it. They studied her address book for potential leads. Rumors that Ruth had testified at a narcotics trial opened up the possibility of revenge as a motive.

By mid-May, troubles within the investigation itself were coming to light. Lieutenant Les Bauman, the acting detective chief, gave a statement that revealed conflicting ideas about the case. The coroner and pathologist disagreed on the time of death. The cause of death, which was thought to have been a broken neck caused by the beating, was then

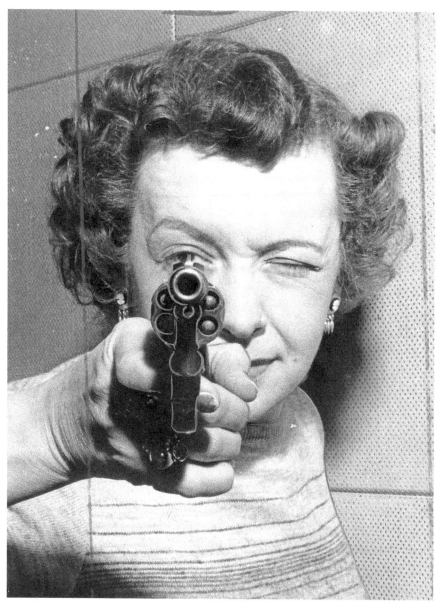

Detective Madeleine Baker. *Courtesy of the* Columbus Citizen-Journal, *Scripps-Howard Newspapers/Grandview Heights Public Library/Photohio.org.*

looking more like strangulation. The two pearl buttons were no longer considered evidence, but the lieutenant did not elaborate on the reasoning behind this.

Those controversies fell by the wayside as police zeroed in on George Phillips, a twenty-three-year-old insurance salesman with a blue car. He had been questioned twice before about the murder and had been under surveillance for two days. The police brought him into custody and subjected him to a three-hour-long lie detector test. Phillips had been connected to Ruth Alter through her former workplace, the Broad-Hague Restaurant. The restaurant was owned by Phillips's family. Neighbors and a salesman who worked in the area were called in to identify Phillips and his car. He was charged with first-degree murder. Phillips pleaded not guilty.

The evidence against him was simultaneously promising and problematic. Witnesses had seen a "late-model" blue car in the neighborhood on the morning of the murder. Phillips drove a 1939 blue car. The general body shape of cars became much sleeker around 1947. It would have been hard to mistake Phillips's car for a late model. The salesman who was seen at the Alters' door was described as a short, stocky man in a light blue suit and carrying a briefcase, and it was said he probably had a mustache. That fit Phillips, although none of the witnesses had noted that the man was one-armed. Phillips had lost his right arm from the elbow down in an accident when he was a toddler. Phillips did have a mustache on the day of the murder that he had shaved off a couple of weeks later. The blood that was found in his car, suit, briefcase and the soles of his shoes was first explained away by a cut on his hand, but he later said it was from a chicken slaughterhouse he had been to. He denied making a call to the Alter home several days before the murder. Russell Alter said that he had made two calls to them. Phillips claimed that he had never visited the Alter home. Witnesses said that they had seen him there on May 5. His business card was found at the vestibule of the Alter home. He gave confused information about his whereabouts on the day of the murder. He said that he had been on his debit route around 10:30 a.m., after being in the office since 8:00 a.m., but policy holders who had been interviewed said that he started at 1:00 p.m.

Motive was another matter of contention. The police knew Ruth had struck him once during an argument in the restaurant where she used to work. They toyed with the idea that the incident may have had something to do with the murder. In their scenario, Phillips had come to the Alter home to sell the family insurance for their new baby. Phillips, who was known to make teasing remarks, may have said something to anger Ruth, setting off an argument that turned suddenly violent.

Phillips was living with his uncle Gus Sora and grandmother Dora Sora. His family believed that he was being framed. They questioned the fact that the hairs found in Ruth's hand were gray while George's hair was jet black. His uncle described him as a "jolly, over talkative" young man who was well liked.[49] He defended him as "not the brutal type" and denied that Phillips was quick-tempered.[50] Phillips's grandmother saw his clothes before they were taken away by the police. She protested that there had been no bloodstains on them at that point. She was the one who nagged him to shave off his mustache because she thought it made him look too old.

Others who knew him were equally doubtful about the allegations made against him. Phillips's employer found it unlikely that he had attempted to sell insurance to Ruth by himself. It was customary for new employees, such as Phillips, to have a senior insurance representative present during sales calls. His supervisor said that the accused had asked the assistant district manager to accompany him to talk to Ruth. Both friends and coworkers noted that Phillips's "light-hearted and carefree" demeanor never changed after the murder.[51]

Phillips's family retained former lieutenant governor Paul M. Herbert as his attorney. Herbert alleged that the police released a lot of information to turn the public against Phillips out of desperation. Herbert stated, "To endeavor to save an innocent man is the reason why I am representing him."[52]

Information against Phillips continued to dribble out to the newspapers. Lieutenant Les Bauman said that while Phillips would normally contact twelve clients a day, he did not contact any of the twelve on his list for the day on the day of the murder. A partial fingerprint was found in the blood on the floor that did not match anyone who had previously been questioned in the case, although Bauman would not confirm if it matched Phillips's fingerprints. Bauman reported that they found a note in Phillips's personal effects that said, "Alter. Latter part of April. His home."[53] Police claimed that his business card was found on the stoop of the Alter home. Four witnesses attested to having heard him make a call to Ruth to make an appointment. Police disclosed that staff at the laundry where Phillips had his clothes cleaned noticed bloodstains on the left side of the shirt before they washed it.

Information then came out that there were fingermarks around Ruth's neck. The police were quick to point out that those could have been made by Phillips, regardless of the fact that he only had one arm. The young man was very athletic. His lack of an arm did not keep him from being an avid bowler and tennis player.

Attorney Paul Herbert began his own campaign to clear Phillips in the minds of the public. He told the newspapers that witnesses contacted him to say that Phillips had visited them to collect insurance premiums on the day of the murder. They were certain of the time he was there. Coworkers verified that Phillips had been with them most of the morning. After a meeting that included new hire Phillips, they went to a restaurant for coffee and donuts, not returning until 11:15 a.m. Another client had a receipt written by Phillips that showed he had been there around 11:55 a.m. Herbert said that the business card at the Alter home was one that Phillips had previously given to Russell in person at a West Side restaurant. He suggested that the card had been "planted" at the Alter home. He brought up complaints that police had questioned Phillips for ten hours straight and tried to threaten him into a confession.

Judge Charles Petree set the preliminary hearing for May 29. In the end, Phillips was bound over to the grand jury without bond for the first-degree murder charge. A couple of months later, the Franklin County grand jury indicted Phillips on a lower charge of second-degree murder. That eliminated the threat of the death sentence. If found guilty of the second-degree murder charge, Phillips faced a maximum penalty of life in prison but could be eligible for parole in ten years. His bail was reduced to $25,000 to be more in line with what was typically required for second-degree murder suspects.

In preparation for the trial, Bartlett had Ruth's body exhumed from her grave at the Rose Hill Cemetery in Roseville. The purpose of this was kept secret. Observers noticed that Bartlett and Dr. Evans were paying particular attention to her face.

The trial started on October 23. It was long, convoluted and, in the opinion of the spectators, rather boring. Much of it felt like repeated cases of "he said, she said."

Throughout the preliminary hearing, the grand jury hearing and the trial itself, many of the same issues were brought up. The most concerning of these were the lack of clarity on the time and manner of death and the mishandling of physical evidence.

The time of death proved to be a moving target. In a pretrial disclosure to the defense, Bartlett had stated that Ruth was killed between 8:35 a.m. and 6:15 p.m., but the exact hour of her death was unknown. Dr. Evans then asserted that the time of death was around noon, not 6:00 a.m., as had been reported at the time of the autopsy, or 9:00 a.m., as he had claimed in the pretrial hearing. Later, under cross-examination, Dr. Evans said that the time of death would have been ten to twelve hours before he viewed her body at 9:30 p.m. at University Hospital. That would have put the time of death between 9:30 and 11:30 a.m. Dr. Robert E. Wybel, the pathology instructor at Ohio State University who performed the autopsy on Ruth, placed the time of death at around 1:00 p.m., plus or minus two hours.

A witness's testimony suggested that the murder had taken place at the earlier end of Wybel's time frame. A.J. Churches, a county building inspector, said that he had called at the Alter home between 11:45 a.m. and noon. No one came to the door when he knocked. He was there to check on a new building permit for the Alters' next-door neighbor, Mr. Post, and had mistakenly gone to the wrong address. He testified that while the storm door was closed, the front door was open by about a foot. He heard no noise from inside the house. He also knocked at the back, again receiving no response.

Wybel stated that the cause of death was strangulation. Ruth had been beaten about the head and had a broken nose and multiple lacerations. There were marks on both sides of her neck. Her left hyoid bone was crushed. Herbert called into question the fingernail marks on her neck and the matter of Phillips only having one arm, his left one. Wybel could not definitively say whether they were made by a right hand, left hand or both, and he could not say if the scratches were made by finger or thumbnails. Dr. John T. Paugh, who assisted Dr. Wybel, agreed with Dr. Wybel's assessment that it could not be determined which hand—or if both hands—were used to strangle Ruth.

More questions were raised about the missing strands of hair. Herbert threatened Dr. Robert Evans with a perjury investigation over his claims that he knew nothing about the gray hairs found in Ruth's hands. In addition to the original findings by Dr. Emmerick Von Haam, two more pathologists at the Ohio State University Hospital who performed Ruth's autopsy said that they had found fifty hairs clutched in her hands. Dr. Wybel emphasized that he tried to give them to Evans three times as possible evidence, only to be told by the coroner that the man who did it was already locked up. Dr. Paugh concurred that Dr. Evans was adamant that a woman could not have committed the crime the two times he heard Dr. Wybel suggest the idea.

Wybel characterized the strands of hair as seeming to be those of a woman—six inches long and light brown or blond with part of each strand being gray. He compared the strands to Ruth's hair, which he determined was slightly darker than the average brown. He found the color of the strands and Ruth's hair to be "markedly different."[54] After Evans's dismissal of the evidence, the hair was placed on a table and was probably discarded when the room was cleaned the next morning. Herbert asked him why he did not keep the hairs if he felt that they were evidence. He responded that he accepted Dr. Evans's authority on that, so he left the hairs on the autopsy table. Bartlett pushed him on that, saying that Wybel's boss, Dr. Emmerick Von Haam, emphasized that the autopsy's purpose was to preserve evidence. Wybel agreed.

The hair was not the only evidence to go missing. Police Chemist Lloyd Shupe testified that clothing from the case was removed from the evidence cabinet while he was on vacation.

Bartlett tried to convince the jury that the discarded hairs found clutched in Ruth's hand were her own. Dr. Evans testified that when Ruth's body was exhumed, her hair was found to be 50 percent gray. He asserted that a pathological report made shortly after her killing was incorrect in describing her hair as brown. Evans again denied knowledge of the missing hairs. He did admit that someone had mentioned the hairs to him—probably on the night the autopsy was performed. Herbert pointed out that Ruth's hair had been described as hennaed before her death and had been washed by the undertaker. Russell described her hair as brown but said that it had recently started to go gray. She had gone to the hairdressers frequently before the baby was born.

A key piece of evidence against Phillips, the identification of his car at the scene of the crime, was another point of contention during the trial. Emma Russell, a neighbor from directly across the street, testified that Phillips's confiscated blue-gray suit, briefcase and car looked similar to the ones she saw in front of the Alter house on the day of the murder. Unlike her testimony at the time, in which she claimed that the car was a "late-model" blue Chevrolet, she then said that it was a 1939 or 1940 blue Pontiac like the one Phillips drove. She said that it had been partially blocking her driveway and drove away around 9:30 a.m. She became aware of the man and the car because she had heard a knocking on her door while she was in the back of her house. By the time she got to the door, she saw a man heading over to the Alters' house. She observed a gas meter reader walking on the Alters' driveway around noon.

Under cross-examination by Herbert, Emma clarified that she had only seen the man at the Alter vestibule from the back and had not noticed an

A comparison of car body shapes in 1939 (*top*) and 1951 (*bottom*). © *Randomshot | Dreamstime (top) and Photodynamx | Dreamstime (bottom).*

empty sleeve flopping despite the fact that it was a windy day. She had known George Phillips for about ten years and did not identify him in the lineup as the man she had seen at the Alters' home. When asked if a neighbor had identified someone in the lineup, she said yes. Herbert pointed out that the man identified was a city detective. Emma testified that while Phillips's briefcase was like the one she had seen the man carrying, it was a different color. She also conceded that she could not identify the makes of the cars owned by her neighbors.

Neighbor Ruth Ward found the blue car and the man at the Alters' door suspicious enough to write down the license plate number. It did not match that of Phillips's car. When she was taken to the police station twenty-three weeks later, Phillips's car was parked separately from the other cars. She identified it as the one she saw. During the suspect lineup, she recognized Phillips as a man she had seen at the Alters' house the day before the murder. She explained that while he resembled the man who was there the day of the murder, Phillips was not that man.

The mystery of the blue car may have been solved by insurance salesman Elmer F. Gatts. He testified that his 1949 blue Pontiac had been parked across the street from the Alters' house between 11:00 a.m. and noon that day. He said that he had been given a message to pick up an insurance claim there. Gatts noted that the storm door was open. He went into the vestibule, but no one answered the door when he knocked.

The bloodstains found in Phillips's car could not be proven to have come from the murder scene. Pathologist Dr. Horace B. Davidson said that the blood found on the pedal of Phillips's car was not in a condition that would allow it to be typed. Phillips's mechanic, who sold the car to Phillips and who had worked on it after he bought it, accounted for the blood in the car, as he said it had come from an unstaunched finger injury that he had at the time he worked on the car. One of the repairs required him to work under the dashboard.

The claims that a bloodied men's shirt had been sent to a laundry the day after the murder were under scrutiny. Lucille Wood stopped working for the Abbott Laundry and Dry Cleaning Company on Sullivant Avenue two days after the murder. She recalled that a bloodstained shirt had been brought in for cleaning shortly before her last day there. According to the records of the cleaner's bookkeeper, laundry had been picked up from Phillips's home the day after the murder. Wood identified a shirt that was presented as part of the state's evidence as one she had marked to be treated for bloodstains. It was brought up during the cross-examination that the laundry frequently got bloodstained shirts from employees of Southwest Poultry, which was just down the street.

There were discrepancies between what the police said Phillips had told them and Phillips's own testimony. Sergeant James Potts quoted Phillips as saying, "I will tell the whole story," when he had been taken into custody.[55] He claimed that Phillips said that he left for his debit route no later than 10:45 a.m. That was inconsistent with the statements from Phillips's coworkers who said he had been with them in a meeting until 11:00 and then went out with them for a bite to eat. Potts testified that Phillips had denied making telephone calls to the Alters' home. Lieutenant Les Bauman asserted that Phillips had told him he had visited the Alter home, but no one was there. He said that Phillips originally denied making a phone call to the Alter home from a client's apartment but later admitted to it. Bauman contradicted himself by saying that Phillips could not account for his time on the day of the murder and then later mentioning that Phillips had named several homes he went to pick up insurance receipts.

Phillips acknowledged that he may have told the police some of that. He explained that after hours of being grilled by the police, he was having trouble remembering things. He was questioned by several policemen for twelve hours on the second day he was brought in. At least one of the claims made by the police was disproven. Frances Helmbrecht, who was the stenographer present during Phillips's interrogation by the police, confirmed from her notes that Phillips never said that he would "tell the whole story" to his interrogators.[56] Phillips also denied saying it.

He admitted that he had phoned the Alters before the murder but probably did tell the police that he hadn't. He said that he didn't remember making the call until they told him where it had been made from. He had spoken to Ruth on the phone a couple of times about insurance the Tuesday before the murder. She referred him to her husband, as he was the one who made those decisions.

Phillips explained that the "fight" between him and Ruth at his father's restaurant was more good-natured than it had been previously presented as. He recounted that he had cheekily greeted her one morning with, "Hi, tubby!"[57] She laughingly kicked him. He gave her a push in return. He described her as a conscientious, hard worker who liked to have the upper hand.

Bartlett got Phillips to acknowledge that some of the insurance calls he claimed to have made on April 25 had actually been made on other days. Phillips maintained that he had shaved his mustache off before the murder—not in early May as the police insisted he had. He said he grew it to look older but had difficulty keeping it trimmed. He said that he was not able to afford a briefcase, so he used an old school notebook. He identified the brown "briefcase" that the state had presented as evidence as his notebook.

After three hours of deliberation, the jury acquitted Phillips. Their explanation for the decision was that there was too much doubt. Two jury members remarked that key points in the state's case—the blood in Phillips's car and his clothing—had reasonable alternative explanations. Sheriff Ralph J. Paul called the acquittal a miscarriage of justice. Unwilling to dismiss Phillips as the murderer, the police stated they would probably not pursue the case further unless new evidence presented itself. It never did.

7

THE RED SHOE MYSTERY

I t seemed like an ordinary Saturday morning on February 23, 1946, when Lola Celli left her Grandview Heights home to go shopping downtown. It became anything but.

Looking back, the weekend had perhaps not gotten off to such an ordinary start. Lola, a twenty-four-year-old home economics teacher at the West Mansfield High School in Logan County, had come home for her weekly visit with her family. This weekend was going to be a long one, starting with President's Day, which, at that time, was celebrated on a Friday. Lola told Mr. and Mrs. L.E. Lybarger, the couple she rented a room from, that she had to get home to Grandview that Thursday night because she had a lot to do. On Friday, when she supposedly had so much to do, all she did was work around the house and read. This was particularly odd, as she had specifically been asked to come home to visit a childhood friend who was in serious condition at the hospital. Lola again had insisted that she was "too busy" and would just send him a card.

On Saturday morning, she told her family that she was going to run some errands downtown and would be home in time for lunch. Her plan was to open a charge account at the Roberts Store on the corner of Gay and High Streets, buy some nylons there and shop for some curtain material for her mother. Next, she intended to visit a jewelry store. She had taken sixty dollars with her for the shopping expenses, which was a little over a week's salary for the average high school teacher at the time.

Lola dressed elegantly in an aqua-colored dress with faint red stripes, red shoes and a gray fur coat and hat to run her errands. She left her house at 10:30 a.m. to catch a bus downtown. Her mother became concerned when the normally prompt Lola had not come back home by 2:00 p.m. Since nylons were often hard to find, the family thought her errands simply may have taken longer than expected. By 6:00 p.m., they had gotten worried. They still hoped that she had run into a girlfriend and lost track of time. An hour later, her brother Felice, a chemical engineer at Ohio State University, began meeting all of the buses coming back from downtown.

Artist's rendering of Lola Celli. *Author's collection.*

Other family members called neighbors and friends. Her father, Michael Celli, was told by a neighbor, Harry Lane, that he had seen her pass by his house as he was rushing to get ready to catch a bus downtown. Lane was a World War II veteran and a student at Franklin University. A few minutes after he left the house, he took a shortcut to Westwood, which was the next stop after the one Lola was headed toward. It took about ten minutes for the bus to arrive. When he boarded, he looked around for Lola, hoping to sit with her. As she had had plenty of time to catch the bus, he was surprised to find that she was not on it.

After the last bus had come from downtown for the evening, Lola's family called the police.

Lola did not seem the type to run off. She had been an honors student both in high school and while attending the Ohio State University. She was a straight arrow who neither smoked nor drank, and she seldom went on dates. She described herself as being someone who might give the first impression of being a flirt, but she was really a homebody. Her brother claimed she was "a perfect girl" who thought it was improper to accept a ride.[58] He surmised that she would have had to have been threatened to get into someone's car. S.Z. Mygrant, the superintendent of the West Mansfield Schools, praised Lola as a young woman "above reproach."[59] He said that she was an exceptional worker and well liked. She did not take advantage of her popularity, only going out with her friend and fellow teacher Pauline Lybarger.

Grandview police, led by Chief Robert P. Livingston, took her disappearance seriously. They had the Roberts Store check its records for the day. No receipts or new charge accounts were found in Lola's name. The police and state highway patrol searched the area's ravines, gullies and railroad tracks. Seven other states got involved in the search.

As the investigation went on, more information poured in that shed a different light on Lola's mental state. Teachers and students at the West Mansfield High School expressed concern that she had been worried and anxious about her teaching progress. They said that she feared that her teaching was not up to snuff and mused that the stress had led to amnesia.

Lola had majored in romance languages with a minor in home economics. She had hoped to be an interpreter for Pan-Am Airlines and put her fluency in five languages to use. Instead, she was offered the teaching position at West Mansfield that paid too well to turn it down. The problem was that the job was to teach home economics and biology. Lola's friend Pauline said that she had so much anxiety about the job that she would wring her hands and fret when making up lesson plans in the evening. Despite her fears, school officials were quite pleased with her work.

One student noted that Lola had severe headaches. Pauline Lybarger confirmed that, saying that Lola had started taking nerve medicine to keep them under control. Lola's family disputed that, however, contending that she was in good health.

Miss Lybarger commented on how thoughtful Lola was. One Friday evening, the train to Columbus was running two and a half hours late, but Lola insisted on waiting for it instead of taking the next train in the morning, as she did not want her mother to worry. She would also call to let her landlords, Pauline's parents, know when she was going to be late coming home from work.

All of her acquaintances in West Mansfield agreed that she was not seeing any men. Her extracurricular activities were all school-related or revolved around spending time with Pauline. Her landlady said that the only man she mentioned was a Dr. Anthony J. Melfi, who had died the day after she disappeared. She and the young Dr. Melfi were friends when she was at Ohio State University. They attended many parties together.

Police questioned Columbus and Southern Ohio Electric Company bus drivers who may have been in the vicinity where Lola was last seen. She typically took the Arlington line. The Fifth Avenue line, which she was said to have disliked, was an alternative route for her. The bus that neighbor Harry Lane caught was on the Arlington line.

The police fielded reports from in and around Columbus from people who claimed to have seen Lola. One individual mentioned seeing a woman fitting Lola's description while waiting for an "owl" streetcar at 4:00 a.m. a few days after her disappearance. The woman, who was described as acting strangely, boarded the car from a shelter on High Street in Clintonville. Another witness claimed they saw Lola enter an automobile shortly after she left her home the morning of her disappearance. The police asked the state highway patrol to check the license number.

Grandview police chief Robert Livingston had his officers search the quarries and banks along the Scioto River. While they found no clues by the Scioto River, a report came in that a Hilltop resident had found a woman's red shoe by the Olentangy River.

In an effort to make a more intensive search of the area, a corps of 175 high school boys from Grandview and Upper Arlington volunteered to comb the area immediately northwest and west of their respective neighborhoods. The students were operating under the direction of Patrolman I.N. Neff of the Grandview Police and Captain J.F. Holt of the Upper Arlington Police Department. They were given clear descriptions of what Lola had been wearing. Two members of the state highway patrol and the Franklin County Sheriff's Department controlled the movement of the students, who were spaced twenty-five feet apart. Aside from a couple of women's handkerchiefs, their efforts again yielded nothing of interest. The Cellis did not recognize any of the handkerchiefs.

When the police interviewed the original man, who reported the red shoe, the case took a sinister turn. Cecil Scott said he found the shoe along the Olentangy River Road north of North Broadway at Thomas Lane. He was driving south along the road when he saw a red Dodge coupe pass. It sounded like there was an argument going on between the man and woman in the car. The woman kicked her feet in the air. Scott noticed that the right door window was broken out. At that point, he turned his car around to follow the slow-moving coupe. The shoe fell out of the window as the car pulled away. Several other people reported seeing the shoe, although police were unable to find it.

The car was also reported as having been seen at a filling station near stop 18 on North High Street. The attendant said the man who was driving the car told a female passenger to keep quiet. The right window of the car, which was a model from 1937 or later, was broken. The man gave the attendant a five-dollar bill to pay for the two dollars' worth of gas and drove off without waiting for change.

A map detail of Grandview Heights, where Lola Celli was last seen. *Courtesy of the Columbus Metropolitan Library.*

As the community collectively worried about the pretty young schoolteacher's safety, a $205 reward was offered for information leading to a solution to the case. The reward was raised by donations from several businessmen, Club 26 and the Nick Caruso Post of the Italian American World War Veterans. The reward was increased to $505 with donations from *The Columbus Dispatch* and the county commissioners.

Rumors and tips began flying in as the police left no stone unturned. Sheriff Earl of Delaware County received reports that a red car had been seen in the vicinity of Twin Lakes, north of the O'Shaughnessy Dam, the day of Lola's disappearance. Between that and a tip that was given to Chief Deputy Sheriff Ralph Garner, the decision was made to drag the Twin Lakes. The search turned up nothing. Another report said that residents in West Jefferson had seen a woman being slapped and stuffed into a car on Saturday night. Police investigated the incident. They came to the conclusion that the people involved were "Saturday night drunks."[60] The Grandview Heights police checked with all of the area convents to see if Lola had sequestered herself in one of them. They examined some women's clothing that was found under the Calumet Street Bridge. It did not match the description of the clothing that Lola was last seen wearing.

The Cellis, likewise, were being contacted with possible information about their daughter. One telephone call in particular stood out. The short call, which came from a West Side drugstore phone booth, was a man's voice telling them not to worry about Lola. He assured the family that she was alive and well and in Columbus. The police dismissed it as a crank call.

Meanwhile, people reported seeing Lola in Ironton, Ohio, on February 27. Carl Hughes, a foreman at a stove repair company, said that he saw her with a man at the Waldo Restaurant around noon. Mrs. Marshall Ankrum of North Kenova almost struck a woman who looked like Lola with her car around 5:00 p.m. that same day. Both identified the women they saw as being Lola when shown a photograph of her. Mrs. Ankrum had notified Chief Robert Livingston by letter about the near accident. Ironton police chief Garland Wileman investigated the report on his behalf.

In a phone interview with *The Columbus Evening Dispatch*, Hughes said that the woman he saw looked exactly like Lola. She caught his attention because she was wearing a distinctive gray fur coat, had a foreign look to her and was pretty. He thought that she had on red shoes. Felice Celli agreed that Hughes's description of the fur on the coat was consistent with the unusual texture of the Bombay lamb coat that his sister was last seen wearing. The specific kind of fur coat she had been wearing had not previously been reported by the newspapers. Hughes said that her companion was a nice-looking man around thirty-five years of age and 140 pounds who was wearing a gray overcoat. The couple seemed relaxed with each other, and the man paid for the meal. Hughes alerted Chief Wileman about the sighting after Lola's photograph appeared in the paper a couple of days later. The Cellis said that Lola had no known friends in the Ironton area, nor did they know of any male acquaintance who fit the man's description.

As time went by, some hope was lost. The Bokescreek Township Board of Education hired a new teacher to replace Lola at the West Mansfield High School. Police dismissed the possibility that Lola had amnesia, citing the idea that she would have been found by then if that was the case.

In late July, Fred Igel, the caretaker at Mount Calvary, received two phone calls from a woman saying that Lola's body had been buried in a cemetery between Columbus and Groveport or, alternately, in a shallow grave near a fence by a hill at Mount Calvary. *The Columbus Evening Dispatch* then received a call from a woman who claimed that Lola had been buried in a grave where a body had been exhumed. The police tracked the calls to a woman who had previously been an inmate at the Columbus State Hospital, which treated psychiatric patients.

The next day, *The Columbus Evening Dispatch* was contacted by a caller who had a happier tale about Lola's fate. The young-sounding man wanted to alleviate the family's fears after the traumatic reports about Lola supposedly being dead. The caller claimed that Lola had run off with him to get married. He said that they were living in a small town near Columbus and were expecting a baby. He had previously called the Celli family two or three times to let them know. Lola's brother Felice admitted that this was possible, but they had received so many phone calls that he couldn't remember. Lola's fifteen-year-old sister, Elda, did take a call earlier in the week from the man who claimed to be Lola's husband. She tried to get identifying information from the man, including his name and where he lived, but he dodged her questions. The Cellis did not know of any man whom Lola might have married, but they believed she was alive.

In light of that, police checked out a lead that said a woman living near Circleville was Lola Celli. The woman was a pregnant newlywed, as the mysterious caller claimed Lola was. The woman looked so much like Lola that her brother Felice thought it was her at first when he was brought there to identify her.

It wasn't until mid-September that Michael Celli revealed he was positive that he had seen his daughter riding in a car on East Long Street in April. The sighting occurred early in the morning as he was on his way in to work. He was so excited about seeing her in the front seat of the car that he forgot to get the license number until it was out of sight. The car was a blueish-green two-seater. Michael was also so focused on his daughter that he did not notice the driver. Police monitored the nearby intersections every morning for over a week to see if they could find the car again. They were not successful. Felice expressed doubt that the woman his father saw was Lola. Despite Michael Celli's claim that he had seen his daughter, police decided to keep the case open.

The leads grew cold for two and a half years until April 1949, when a Columbus woman, then living in California, implicated her former husband in the disappearance of Lola Celli. She informed police that on the day of Lola's disappearance, her husband was acting strangely. Once the news was out, he became angry when his wife talked about the disappearance and stormed out of the room. Not long after, he disappeared as well.

The next month, the case took a bizarre turn. Stanley Jackson was digging a ditch for a septic tank in the 3600 block of Olentangy River Road, the same general area in which the red shoe had been found. About four feet down, he was stunned when his pick cracked what turned out to be a skull. The skeleton had been buried in a sitting position. Upon investigation, police were informed that the area had been filled in three or four years earlier. That corresponded with the time that Lola had disappeared. It led them to believe that the skeleton was likely that of Lola. But a further examination of the bones proved otherwise. According to the coroner, Dr. Robert A. Evans, the bones were at least twenty years old. He speculated that they could have been those of a long-dead American Indian or possibly a specimen discarded by a doctor. He could not say if it they were the bones of a man or a woman.

The Cellis were still holding onto the hope that Lola was alive eight years later. Ida Celli lamented to *The Columbus Evening Dispatch* that Lola was always on her mind. The crank letters and phone calls continued, as did contacts with psychics and detectives who claimed that they could locate Lola. Ida did not mind the ongoing attempts to find Lola but was heartbroken that they all came to naught. Possible sightings of Lola were widespread, ranging from California to New York City. Lola's brother Felice expressed gratitude for the ongoing publicity of the case. He hoped it would someday bring someone to them who truly knew where Lola was. Ida mentioned that Lola had left a blouse pattern cut out in her room that she had planned on sewing the afternoon of her disappearance. She reminisced about how the family had come over from Italy in 1930, when Lola was only nine years old. Lola had not wanted to leave their village and family. Ida pondered whether they would have been better off if they had stayed in Italy. "Whatever happened, it would be better to know."[61]

Ida's hopes were raised again when a former coworker of her husband saw a woman he believed to be Lola in the garment district of Chicago. Grandview police chief Robert Livingston reopened the case. He, along with some newspapermen, traveled to Chicago to stake out the area where the informant had seen her. They spotted her, only to lose her again when she entered one of the buildings near where she had previously been seen. They checked that building and nearby ones, but she remained elusive. Their next step was to show her picture to all of the employers and elevator operators in those buildings. Finally, they found an employer who did recognize her. That victory was short-lived. He identified her as a model of Greek ancestry who was much taller than Lola.

A new tip caused a flurry of excitement in June 1955. Prosecutor Frank Kearns reportedly paid a tipster $210 for information that she had seen Lola working in Richmond, Virginia, the previous summer. She said that she had first seen her in Washington, D.C., a month after her disappearance. The informant claimed she met Lola when she found the young woman crying in the lobby of the YWCA there. When she asked if she could help, the distraught woman told her that she had many problems. The tipster then invited her to dine with her and a few friends. During dinner, the young woman introduced herself as "Lola" and "Miss Celli."[62] The informant only found out about the disappearance when she later moved to Columbus. She was vacationing in Richmond when she saw a woman who looked like Lola working in the lingerie department of a Montgomery Ward store. She said that when she asked the clerk if she was Lola Celli, the clerk became excited, directed her to another staff member and ran off. The tipster returned to Columbus and talked to a Grandview policeman, who apparently never passed the information on to Chief Livingston. The policeman had been relieved of duty in the intervening months. Some doubt was cast on the story, as a source in Richmond pointed out that Montgomery Ward did not have a lingerie department and did most of its sales by mail order. But it still brought hope to the Cellis, who had had some other changes in their household. Only Ida and her son Felice were still living in the house. Elda, the little sister, had grown up and gotten married. Mr. Celli had passed away at the beginning of 1955, when he was only fifty-seven.

The three-day investigation in Richmond turned out to be a bust. The Montgomery Ward store had closed since the alleged sighting. The investigators checked with other nearby stores, but none had knowledge of any employees who fit Lola's description.

The Celli home. *Courtesy of the Franklin County Auditor's Office.*

Mysteries and bodies continued stacking up a few weeks later when another promising tip led authorities to dig up a grave in a cemetery near Plain City. The tipster told Chief Livingston that a body had been buried there under mysterious circumstances. Two men who had been mentioned in the tip verified that they had been paid by a funeral director to help bury a body about four months after Lola disappeared. They did not remember the exact month, but they recalled the corn being about knee high at the time.

There were irregularities involved in the burial. It was done without a legal permit, and the casket that was used was an inexpensive wooden one of a type that was generally used for the destitute. The impromptu gravediggers testified that the funeral director stopped by their farmhouse near the cemetery around dinnertime and asked for help with the burial. A grave had already been dug, but they had to enlarge it to accommodate the casket. That casket had been placed inside of a wooden shipping box. The grave was dug mostly in the walk of the cemetery, extending partially into a plot owned by Charles Ramey. The owner of the plot had not given permission for the burial.

Upon opening the casket, the police were surprised to find that the badly decomposed body in the casket was dressed in men's clothing. The corpse was sent University Hospital, where it was examined by an archaeologist from the Ohio Historical Society, Raymond Baby. Baby, along with pathologist Dr. J.B. Milligan, determined that the body was that of a young man—about nineteen years old—who was six feet, one inch tall; with light brown hair; a long, narrow face; and would have weighed about 195 pounds. They found no signs of violence. The coroner, Dr. Robert A. Evans, surmised that the deceased had died from natural causes. The body had been embalmed. The boy was dressed in a black suit but had no shoes on. The casket fit so tightly that it did not allow room for his hands to be crossed over his chest.

The police, both in Columbus and Madison County, flew into a whirlwind of activity. They scoured old files trying to match the body to other missing persons cases. They did find that rumors had been circulating in the area for years about an illegal burial. A local mortician raised suspicions when he acted irritated during routine questioning about it.

Police tentatively identified the body as Paul Post, a young man who had died of accidental carbon monoxide poisoning from a faulty stove in January 1944. Prosecutor Samuel L. Devine, who had previously worked on the case as an FBI agent, was called by the boy's stepmother, Nola Post. She said that the description fit Paul. Paul's father, Dorman Post, and his mother, Ethel

Post, were not so sure. They said that Paul had been buried beside Roscoe Ramey in his mother's family plot.

In an odd coincidence, Mr. Post said that he had hired a couple of men to dig the grave for his son but that they had made it too narrow. He started digging it wider himself. Two men from the farm next door, the same men who buried the mystery body two and a half years later, came up to the fence to see what he was doing. He hired them to finish the job. It dawned on Devine that the two burials were probably one and the same and that the farmers who helped were likely just mistaken about the date. He figured that the faulty positioning of the grave may have been an error by the original grave diggers, who had also mistakenly dug the grave too small.

Mr. Post noted that his son had one leg shorter than the other. He pointed out that that should be the deciding factor in figuring out if the mystery body was that of his son. He contended that if the body was Paul's, his grave had been moved. The next day, Mr. Post identified the suit and tie that the body was wearing as being the ones his son had been buried in. Dr. Evans officially deemed the body to be that of Paul Post. He closed the case and ordered that the young man be buried legally and properly.

It appeared that the case was finally solved in August 1956, when Marble Cliff marshal John Guy reported that he knew where Lola was. Grandview police chief Robert R. Livingston and Mayor A.K. Pierce found the report credible enough to close the case. Guy did not release specifics, claiming that to do so would break a confidence. Livingston and Pierce agreed that it was acceptable to honor that confidentiality, as there had been no evidence that a crime had been committed. He did tell Pierce that Lola had her reasons for leaving home and that she was then living within three hundred miles of Columbus. The Cellis, who had not been informed of the development by the police, were understandably doubtful. Other officials who had been involved with the case had not been informed either.

The case was reopened a couple of weeks later when Guy admitted that he did not know where Lola was. He said that the earlier report had been greatly exaggerated. He had picked up some promising information over the past few months and thought it might break the case soon.

Chief Livingston confirmed that the case was still open. He emphasized that they wanted to be able to continue to follow any leads that might still crop up. This turned out to be a wise decision. The following year, informants notified police that Lola might be buried in some woods near Morse and Cherry Bottom Roads. The female informant told Sheriff Stacy Hall that she had found a red shoe, khaki pants and disrupted earth that looked like a freshly dug grave in a wooded area near that intersection the day after Lola disappeared. She did not report it at the time because she didn't want to get involved. A small contingent of officials from Columbus and Franklin County investigated the potential crime scene.

The informants were revealed to be Mr. and Mrs. James A. Warehime, who had owned a farm near the site at the time of Lola's disappearance. An orphaned boy they were raising, Charles Colley, found a red shoe, some women's clothing and pants on the farm. They said that they hadn't made the connection between the items and the case until a more recent news article mentioned Lola's red shoes. They reported the findings to their cousin Common Pleas Judge Ralph J. Bartlett. The investigators did find bones buried in a burlap bag there. However, the bones were that of a small mammal, as confirmed by police chemist Lloyd Shupe.

Ida Celli never gave up hope that her daughter would be returned to her alive and well. When she died in 1985, her obituary noted that she was survived by her children: Lola, Felice and Elda. Lola's siblings did eventually lose faith. Her little sister, Elda C. Butler, passed away in 2006. Both Lola and Felice were mentioned as having preceded her in death.

8
THE DOWNWARD SPIRAL

I t is an open secret among hotel workers that deaths happen at their establishments far more often than guests would ever guess. Sometimes, the deaths are the results of natural causes, such as heart attacks in the middle of an adulterous assignation. Sometimes, they are drug-related— like accidental overdoses from a night of partying or sleeping pill suicides by people who did not want to be found by their loved ones. Then there are the murders.

Ada Reynolds, a housekeeper at the Deshler Hotel, could attest to this fact when she went to clean room 305 on Friday, January 12, 1917. Instead of the usual unmade beds and dirty towels, she found the room strewn with four empty whiskey bottles—but that was the least of her problems. Halfway under the bed was the body of a young woman, her face buried in a pool of blood.

Coroner Louis M. Herskowitz determined that the deceased had died of a bullet wound to her right jaw and a knife wound behind her left ear. The only clues about her identify were her inexpensive suit and a brown hat that bore labels from local shops. Officer Glenn E. Kemp recognized the hat as belonging to a local street walker. The shops themselves could offer no help, except to say that the coat was something they had sold several years before.

The victim's companion for the evening and probable murderer was likewise a mystery. The room was registered to a "C.V. Van Brunt" of Chicago, although authorities in Chicago could find no record of him.[63] H.B. Wilbur, the clerk who registered the enigmatic Van Brunt, remembered him requesting a room high up in the hotel that cost no more than $2.50 a night. After being informed that no rooms fitting those requirements were available, the man said he would take whatever he could get. Despite the oddness of the request, Wilbur could not recall what the man looked like.

The room itself provided the barest of clues. The whiskey was not from the hotel and had likely been bought at a saloon. The police also found a newspaper on the floor. From that, they deduced that the crime would have occurred late Thursday, as a murderer was unlikely to casually go out and buy the evening paper after committing such a heinous act. The newspaper was emblazoned with the story of a suicide attempt by Harry K. Thaw. They momentarily considered the possibility of suicide—inspired by the Thaw story—but quickly dismissed it. The victim's wounds told a different story.

The murderer took the time to wash his hands after the act, leaving blood on the towels and in the washbasin. Aside from a toothbrush, he took all his belongings with him—this included the two keys needed to open each room at the Deshler Hotel. They did find a special skeleton key, the kind burglars used, in the victim's stocking.

The guests in the rooms on either side of the murder site had not heard any gunshots or unusual sounds while they were in the area. A questionable source reported that the hotel bookkeeper had been alerted that a woman was being bothered by a drunken man on the third floor. That story could not be confirmed.

Things moved quickly to ascertain who both the victim and the murderer were. Based on Officer Kemp's recognition of the victim as a known prostitute, Grace Snapp was called in to see if she could identify the woman. As a matron for the Columbus Police Department, Snapp dealt with the hundreds of wayward women who passed through the police station every year. Snapp immediately recognized the victim as Mona Simon. Simon stood out in Snapp's mind because three months prior to the murder, Mona had nearly broken her fingers by slamming an iron door on them. Regardless of the injury done to her, Snapp pitied the young woman.

The next day, Thomas D. Daily, the assistant sports editor of the *Ohio State Journal*, tipped off Police Chief Carter about the identity of the murderer. He saw a newspaper report that a man named C.V. Van Brunt had murdered a woman at the Deshler Hotel. As it happened, Daily had spoken a few days earlier to a twenty-three-year-old Weldon H. Wells, whose mother was close friends with his mother. Wells told Daily that he was staying at the Deshler under the name of "Van Brunt." Wells explained to Daily that he was using an alias because he was running away from a woman in Kansas City.

Artist's rendering of Mona Simon. *Author's collection.*

Wells was charged with the first-degree murder of Mona Simon. The next step was to get him back from Huntington, Indiana, where he had fled. Governor James M. Cox sent Sergeant Peter Albanese of the Columbus Police Department and Franklin County's assistant prosecuting attorney Robert J. O'Donnell to Indianapolis to extradite Wells. Wells said that he would go willingly to prove his innocence. He admitted to having occupied the room where Simon was found until noon on Thursday. He claimed that he never met Simon and that she must have been killed after he vacated the room.

Police in Huntington, Indiana, found Wells at this grandparents' home. In his traveling bag, they discovered a .38-caliber gun, the same type used to kill Mona Simon, and a red-stained coat, undershirt, collar and handkerchief. Wells brushed off the stains, saying they had come from a lip paint he kept in his bag. The police believed them to be bloodstains. Wells later changed his story to say that the stain on his collar was from cutting himself while shaving. He said that stains on his coat were from the paint.

Wild theories about the motive for the murder started to circulate. One suggested that Wells killed Simon after she belatedly informed him that she had a contagious disease. Another was that he killed her in self-defense. The latter theory was proposed by Simon's friends, who noted that she would often cry out that she "must see blood" when she was under the influence of alcohol or drugs.[64] Questions were raised about whether the gun the police found actually belonged to Simon instead of Wells.

Wells was hardly the soul of innocence. Daily described him as having a violent temper. He gave the example of an incident in which he had to stop an angry Wells from stabbing a woman with a pitchfork. While Wells claimed that he had registered at the hotel under the name of Van Brunt to avoid detection by Gladys Wilson of Kansas City, his criminal activity seemed to be a more likely motivation. He was wanted for embezzlement in Kansas City from the brokerage firm of Ward Brothers Wholesale Produce Company. He had taken several checks from Ward Brothers when he left the company's employ on January 4. Either remorse or a fear of getting punished for this crime gave Wells second thoughts. When he passed through Huntington on his way to Columbus, he mailed the checks back to the brokerage.

Charles Ward of Ward Brothers Wholesale Produce Company elaborated on that part of the story. Wells quit Ward Brothers without notice. The company had no idea that he had left its employ until he failed to show up for work the next day. The company traced him to Chicago the day after that. Ward later received a letter from Wells, who was returning the stolen checks. Wells warned him not to bother trying to track him down, as he intended to flee to Canada and join the royal guard. Ward doubted that, as Wells did not have the funds to make it that far. He mentioned that Wells was married but was apparently separated, his wife living in a different state.

Wells had grown up in Huntington, Indiana. His father, a train dispatcher, died when he was young. His mother remarried and moved to Kansas City with her new husband, Claude Benfer. Back in Kansas City, Wells's mother hysterically decreed that her son was innocent. His stepfather gave the more lukewarm assurance that Wells was not "mentally responsible" enough for murder.[65]

Delia M. "Mother" Hubbard, whom Mona Simon stayed with when she first came to Columbus five years earlier, filled the police in on her background. When Simon lived with Hubbard, she was a hardworking, pretty young woman with a promising future. Her weak spot was her bad temper. After a particularly bad spat, Simon moved out. Hubbard was relieved to see her go. When Hubbard ran into her later, she found that Simon had started to drink and run around with men. Simon promised Hubbard that she would try to change her ways, but she never managed to.

Charlotte Martin, a juvenile court officer who had previously worked with Associated Charities, told a similar story. Martin met Simon when she was laid up in the infirmary hospital. Her injury, a broken leg, occurred during a drinking spree. Again, Simon declared that she wanted to clean up her life. She moved to Canton to break ties with her old ways. Simon's compulsion to use booze and cocaine proved to be too much; she was soon back in Columbus and back to her self-destructive habits.

A more sympathetic account of Mona Simon's tragic life appeared in *The Columbus Evening Dispatch*. Simon had been the daughter of a respected sheriff of Barbour County, West Virginia, W.T. Simon. After the death of her parents, Simon sought work in Phillipi, West Virginia, where she became a telephone operator. It was during her time there that her Sunday school teacher Mamie Mason took her on a trip to Columbus. The small-town girl whom Mason remembered as being devout was in awe of the glamor of the big city.

Back in West Virginia, Simon married a man whom *The Columbus Evening Dispatch* described as "not of the sort of her own people."[66] The marriage was not a happy one. It was hinted that Simon may have picked up her drinking and drug use habits from her husband. Things came to a head when Simon's husband shot her. This earned him a jail sentence. He moved to Cincinnati after being released several years later. Although their marriage was effectively over, the pair never officially divorced.

Shattered by the horror her marriage had turned into, Simon fled to the shiny new hope that Columbus represented. After leaving Hubbard's home, Simon moved into the Virginia Hotel. It was then that the lure of alcohol promised to help her forget her woes and drew her in. She became a habitué of the local "grills," accepting food and drinks from men who expected sexual favors in return. The quality of the bars she frequented dropped from decent places where "persons of means" were found to dives filled with criminals.[67] Simon found legitimate work, but her drinking habits caused her to lose her jobs as quickly as she got them. She slipped more and more into prostitution as a way of supporting herself. At the same time, she became more dependent on drugs to make life bearable. This backfired, as the periods in which she was coming down from the drugs made her lows even lower.

Simon's brother Charles H. Simon of Grafton, West Virginia, made multiple trips to Columbus to try to get Simon to turn her life around. His many attempts at rehabilitation ultimately failed. Charles said that he was not surprised when he got the call from Undertaker Osman that she had died a violent death.

Simon was unconcerned about her repeated court appearances and stays in jail. During her final stay of fifteen days during the second half of December, Simon was so low that it did not bother her to be spending Christmas in jail. The alternative, walking the cold streets and picking up men to have sex with for money, was not any more appealing.

People in Simon's hometown of Phillipi remembered her as a cheery-voiced telephone operator who was basically a good young lady but had a hot temper. They expressed concern that her job as a telephone operator exposed her to wealthy men. Those who knew Simon feared that she, in her loneliness, was too dazzled by the dandies to understand that they only saw her as a plaything.

Simon's murder took a toll on a couple of the Deshler Hotel employees. Manager A.H. Carling was bedridden from the stress of it all. Charles Chisholm, the doorman, was dismissed after it was found that he had not

The Columbus City Prison, where Mona Simon was a frequent inmate. *Courtesy of the Columbus Metropolitan Library.*

informed management when he saw Wells sneaking Simon in through a back door. Chisolm told reporters that both Wells and Simon were a bit tipsy and that Simon was not dressed in the usual standards of a typical Deshler guest. Wells also realized that she was not their typical clientele, so he instructed her to take the stairs while he took the elevator and said they would meet on the third floor.

A witness who had seen Wells with Simon before they left for the Deshler had also commented on Simon not being the Deshler Hotel type. The witness said that Simon appeared shocked when Wells suggested that they go to his room at the hotel. She knew that the place was ritzier than she was used to and that she would be out of place there.

A night in jail gave Wells time to reconsider his story. He then confessed to the police in Huntington, Indiana, that he may have killed Mona Simon but that he had been too drunk at the time to remember it. He excused himself, saying that if he did it, it was because he was crazy from the booze.

Mrs. C.D. Benfer, Wells's mother, declared that her son was insane. She related a story from two years before when he had made a trip to Chicago. She received a telegram saying that he had been killed. Upon investigation, it turned out that Wells himself had sent the telegram. She intended to hire an attorney to aid him in an insanity defense. Again, his stepfather gave a lackluster account of the young man. He said that Wells couldn't keep a job for very long, despite having had many good positions. He painted Wells as a heavy drinker who got into "several girl scrapes."[68]

A man named William Davis told Columbus police that Mona Simon had lived with him four years before her death. According to him, Wells visited the house and threatened her. Thomas Daily, the only person in Columbus who seemed to know Wells, could not confirm that Wells had ever been in Columbus before.

Funeral services were held for Simon in the undertaking rooms of O.H. Osman on West Broad Street. So many people showed up to pay their respects that the room was packed. Many appeared to be denizens of demimonde that Simon had been a part of in her last years. Her remains were scheduled to be sent back to Grafton, West Virginia, the following day. Four of Simon's six siblings were awaiting the arrival of her body for burial. Two of her brothers shared Mona's wanderlust and could not be located.

The coverage of the case caused an uproar among readers of the newspapers, resulting in a flurry of letters to the editor. Some readers were angry at the amount of coverage the case had been given. They did not feel that a woman whose actions had led to her own fall from respectability warranted any sympathy. One reader went so far as to accuse her long-dead mother of causing her plight through neglect. Just as many readers expressed concern that society did not step in to help wayward women like Simon before they reached such tragic ends. They emphasized that hundreds of young, single women came to Columbus every year in search of work. Without community support, they feared that those women would likewise drift into the wine rooms out of loneliness, boredom or a need to supplement the income from their low-paying jobs. Others pushed for publicly funded treatment centers for alcoholism and drug abuse. They pointed out that while there were private clinics for that, people like Simon could not afford them. Members of the temperance movement blamed the saloons themselves for Simon's downfall.

The Columbus Evening Dispatch announced that since it had covered the Simon murder case so thoroughly, it would pare back its coverage of the trial itself. It declined to cover "salacious details," stating it did not wish to make innocent people look evil.[69]

Once he returned to Columbus, Wells waived his right to a preliminary hearing in a municipal court. He pleaded not guilty, claiming that he had

THE DESHLER

The Deshler Hotel. *Courtesy of the Columbus Metropolitan Library.*

killed Mona Simon in self-defense. Judge Edward F. Berry bound him over to the grand jury without bond.

Wells made a full confession to the police. *The Columbus Evening Dispatch* remarked that many parts of the confession were too tawdry to report. Wells's version of events said that he left the hotel at 8:30 in the evening to take a walk. He was then "accosted" by Simon, whom he claimed to have never seen before.[70] She then led him to a saloon in an alley near the train tracks several blocks from the hotel. He called the saloon a "colored joint" and said was too afraid of the men there to enter.[71] Wells then suggested that they go up to his room at the Deshler Hotel instead. Once there, he was appalled by how "shabby" Simon looked.[72] He tried to get her to leave, but when she threatened to make a scene, they went up the elevator to his room. After Wells partook of Simon's professional skills, she allegedly threatened to cut him with a razor. He became fearful and brought out his revolver. She bit him, causing him to shoot her in return. At another point, he changed his story, saying that he shot her after she had made an upsetting confession to him.

Either way, he washed the blood off his hands in a daze. Scooping his belongings into his travel bag, he quietly left the room. He slipped into the lobby, leaving his keys on the registration desk while the clerk was busy. He headed to a nearby saloon to get a drink of whiskey. Then he then made a beeline to Union Station and caught the next train to Indianapolis. From there, he made his way to his grandmother's house in Huntington.

When asked why he did not use his revolver on the Huntington police when they came to arrest him, he gave a peculiar answer. He said that he thought that they were there to arrest him for embezzlement, not for the murder.

The police had their doubts about Well's story. Based on the physical evidence in the room, they found it unlikely that Simon had been standing up when she was shot. If anything, the bloodstains on the bed suggested that she had been sleeping and that Wells used a pillow and the bed covers to muffle the sound of the gunshot. Considering how much the physical evidence contradicted his version of events, they expected him to plead guilty and throw himself on the mercy of the court before the end of his trial. Wells revised his account yet again to say that Simon was indeed on the bed when he shot her.

Wells was indicted on first-degree murder charges on March 7. Former attorney general Timothy S. Hogan was retained to represent him. Emmet Tompkins was to be his other defense attorney. Once the trial opened on Monday, May 14, it proceeded rapidly. By noon on Tuesday, the state had already put most of its witnesses on the stand. It concentrated on testimony regarding the crime scene. The defense had subpoenaed only half as many witnesses as the prosecution had. *The Columbus Evening Dispatch* noted that women seemed to be especially interested in the case. The majority of the spectators at the trial were female.

The state closed its case at noon on Wednesday. Wells took the stand, talking about his early life as well as the night of the murder. He claimed that he had accidentally shot Simon while trying to prevent her from pulling out a razor he believed she had concealed on her person. The defense, likewise, made short work of the trial. It closed its case Thursday morning, after bringing forth a few witnesses to testify about Simon's character. The witnesses—Anna Behm, a night matron at the city prison; Grace Snapp, the day matron there; and former matron of the county jail, Mrs. William Slack—all testified that Simon had a quarrelsome, violent nature. Judge Edgar B. Kincaid was not impressed. He announced that he was considering withdrawing the plea of self-defense.

On May 19, after three hours of deliberation, the jury returned a guilty verdict and convicted Wells on a charge of second-degree murder. This verdict carried an automatic sentence of life in prison. Judge Kincaid acknowledged that the jury returned the correct verdict. He added that if, at some point in the future, Wells showed that he had truly reformed, the judge would reconsider.

Judge Kincaid later made good on his word. He, along with nine of the jury members and Prosecuting Attorney Hugo Schlesinger, made a case to the board of clemency that Wells had indeed reformed. They were confident that the hard work and discipline of being in the penitentiary had matured the previously alcoholic, self-indulgent young man. This faith in his reformation was backed up by Ward Brothers, which agreed to give him a second chance. On the recommendation of the board, Governor A.V. Donahey commuted Wells's sentence to ten years. Wells was released on September 28, 1923. He had been given further time off for good behavior, making his time spent in the penitentiary a mere six years and four months. Wells returned to Kansas City and then went on to work in sales in San Francisco.

9

THE SPURNED SUITOR

On the surface, it looked like life was going well for Margaretta "Gretchen" Seeling. Just two months shy of her twentieth birthday, she had established herself as a hired girl in the household of Colonel Charles Parrott. Her employers were the best one could hope for. They had grown to trust and love her for her industrious nature and pleasant disposition. The work was hard, but the setting was a dream come true. The Parrotts' elegant mansion sat beside Trinity Lutheran Church and was right across the street from the Ohio Statehouse. What young woman wouldn't want to be right in the heart of the vibrant city?

Gretchen was quite lovely herself, with flaxen hair, a pretty face and a fashionable figure. While being beautiful wasn't the most important thing in the world, it did come with some advantages. A fruit vendor might gift her with an extra apple when she shopped at Central Market. Strangers were more likely to give a friendly nod as she passed by. She had a better chance of getting a desirable position as a parlor maid if she ever tired of working for the Parrotts. But there were disadvantages—one of them was Frederick Greiner.

Gretchen had loved Frederick once. Both immigrants from Germany, they had independently come to the United States a few years earlier. Columbus was where they got to know each other, and they formed a deep attachment there. Gretchen's relatives did not share her admiration of him. They warned her away from him, saying that the twenty-four-year-old carpenter had left Germany because he was wanted for murder there. Gretchen listened. When

The Parrot Mansion, located to the right of Trinity Lutheran Church. *Courtesy of the Columbus Metropolitan Library.*

he proposed, she turned him down. The more she spurned him, the more desperate he became to make Gretchen his own. His inability to accept her decision began to terrify her. She became increasingly anxious, to the point that it was unbearable. Gretchen confided in her aunt Lizzie Schleier, whom she was living with on Mohawk Street. She told Schleier that she intended to leave the city to get away from him.

She did not leave soon enough. The following morning, September 5, 1884, Greiner forced the issue. Around 7:00 a.m., he came to her workplace and made one last appeal for her hand in marriage. Again, she turned him down. With two shots from his revolver, he made sure that she would never say no to him again.

Colonel Parrott heard the shots and the quickly silenced screams of a woman. He rushed to the basement room where the shots had come from. There, he found Greiner standing with a gun in his hand near a gravely wounded Gretchen. Parrott recognized Greiner from the unwelcome visits he had paid Gretchen there. He grabbed a chair and ran after the fleeing killer, hoping to use it as a makeshift weapon to subdue the culprit. Greiner wrested the chair away from him and aimed his revolver at Parrott's head. He pulled the trigger twice. When it did not go off, he slammed Parrott in the side of the head with the gun. This loosened Parrott's grip enough to get free of him. Parrott continued the chase and was soon joined by John

McCune and others. Harry B. Jones caught Greiner. With the help of John Logan, Jones was able to hold him until the police wagon arrived.

As more information came out, the story grew uglier. Parrott told reporters that Greiner had been a frequent and unwelcome visitor to the home in the days leading up to the shooting. The night before, Greiner had been at the house until 11:00 p.m., threatening to kill "Maggie"—as Gretchen was also called—if she did not agree to marry him. Gretchen had to ask Colonel Parrott to kick him out. When he showed up again, asking to see the young woman, Parrott naively let him in on the conditions that he behave himself better and that he would only stay for five minutes. Greiner and Gretchen had a heated discussion while standing on the steps from the front terrace that led down to the basement. Greiner became increasingly loud. He followed Gretchen as she started to retreat into the basement. That was when he killed her.

A letter from Greiner, written in German and addressed to Mayor Walcutt, was found lying in the basement. It read:

To Mayor or Chief of Police

I have come to a conclusion to take my life, having had trouble with Mrs. Schleier, the aunt of my beloved. I hope she will go to hell and eternity forever. My love has come to a conclusion to die with me.

My tools are at the Case Manufacturing Company, and I have five days wages coming from there. My clothes are at the boardinghouse of Mrs. Buchholz, no. 649 South Front Street. Please be kind enough to take my clothes and use them to bear the expenses of my burial. Fred Greiner

P.S. Bertie Greiner is my sister. She is necessory [sic] to my death. Address her at Corrodi's Hotel.[73]

If Greiner was expecting any loving support from his sister, he did not get it. Bertie Greiner revealed that he had also frequently abused her and threatened her life. She said that he had a long history of problematic behavior. He was so abusive toward their parents in Wurtemberg, Germany, that their father sent him away. Bertie spoke more on the relationship between her brother and Gretchen. They had met the previous December. They had been in love, but Gretchen's feelings cooled as he became increasingly aggressive. Bertie admitted that her brother had threatened to kill Gretchen and himself over a month before he committed the act.

There were other warning signs. Greiner's landlady, Mrs. Bucholtz, reported that he was a hothead who was known to often carry a gun. The night before the murder, he had come home a little before 2:00 a.m. and fired six shots into the backyard. He was up again at 5:00 a.m., much earlier than usual, saying that he had to attend to some business.

The police found some letters between Gretchen and Greiner that illustrated their relationship. Early in August, Gretchen had traveled to Urbana with the Parrott family for a camp meeting. She sent a letter to Greiner from there that indicated they were still on romantic terms at that time. She wrote about what a lovely time she was having, sprinkling the letter with endearments. She asked him to write her a long letter and to think of her often. Greiner did write a response but did not mail it. In the letter, he suggests that they move to Dayton together.

While in jail, Greiner still insisted that Gretchen had agreed to die with him. He claimed that he had intended to shoot himself to complete the pact but had been disarmed before he could do so. At his arraignment the next morning, he appeared unaffected but well aware of his plight. He pleaded neither guilty nor not guilty, only telling the judge that he wished to have his "trial in a higher court."[74]

Greiner's trial finally got underway on March 16, 1885, with Judge Wylie presiding. It had originally been scheduled for December. The trial had to be postponed when it became clear that Greiner's understanding of English was so poor that he would need to testify in German. Then there were issues finding suitable jurors. The case had been so widely publicized that it was difficult to find any men who did not already believe Greiner to be guilty.

Much of the early part of the trial was a procession of Greiner's acquaintances who either testified for the defense, saying that Greiner was a normal guy, or for the prosecution, saying that he was an irascible young man with a quick temper. One of the more amusing testimonies on the latter count came from a man who had lived at one of the same boardinghouses as Greiner. He thought that Greiner wasn't quite right in the head since he liked to read a lot. The question of whether the witnesses believed Greiner to be sane came up at times.

Colonel Parrott repeated his story, filling in more aspects of it. Greiner had come to see Gretchen the night before he killed her, moping to Parrott that Gretchen did not want to have anything more to do with him. She only reluctantly came downstairs to talk to him, knowing that he refused to leave until she did so. Greiner asked her a question in German, to which she replied, "*Nein.*"[75] On the day of the murder, just after he heard the gunshots,

Parrott ran downstairs to find Gretchen still standing with her hands over her heart and Greiner holding a pistol four or five feet away. Gretchen said that Greiner had shot her and then she collapsed. Greiner started to run up the stairs but came back to fire another shot, this time at Parrott. In the ensuing chase, Greiner ran next door into the yard of Trinity Episcopal Church, where he was caught.

Mary Schumacher told of an odd encounter she had with Greiner when she met him at a wedding. At the event, Greiner had asked if he could borrow one of her husband's guns so that he "could have a little fun" doing target practice.[76] She declined his request.

Gretchen's aunt Mrs. Schleier testified that Greiner had boarded with her for about six months. He was jealous of Gretchen's cousin Charles Koch. On March 26, 1884, at the wedding of another cousin, Greiner threatened, in front of witnesses, to kill both of them if Koch walked Gretchen home. Greiner ended up being her escort. He made comments that if she would not marry him, they would both end up in Green Lawn Cemetery. His threats to kill Gretchen became a frequent occurrence. He mentioned that he "would as soon kill a person as a dog."[77]

Gretchen's aunt kept quiet when Greiner asked her about marrying Gretchen. Gretchen also showed reluctance, saying that they needed to wait a couple of years. Mrs. Schleier said that things had not been good between Gretchen and Greiner for two or three months before the shooting. Gretchen did not wish him ill but did not want to be with him. That situation deteriorated to the point that Gretchen was afraid of him.

As for the story Gretchen's aunt had heard about Greiner having killed a man back in Germany, that had been told to her by Greiner's sister. Gretchen's aunt testified that the sister had spoken about it in front of Gretchen. Gretchen mentioned to witnesses in the Parrott household that she had also heard the story from others. Mrs. Schleier made Greiner find another place to live after he threatened to whip her. She informed her niece of Greiner's threats only after Gretchen had already become afraid of him. She advised Gretchen that it was her choice if she wanted to marry Greiner, but she begged her to be careful.

Bertha Greiner told the jury that she had come to the United States from Germany about a year after her brother had. She had only known Mrs. Schleier and Gretchen for about a year. She denied ever telling either of them that her brother had killed someone in Germany. She was not allowed to answer a question from the defense about whether that rumor was true.

Greiner had boarded with Frances Buchholz three years earlier and had moved back three weeks before the murder. Frances said that when he moved back in, he groused that he was having family trouble and that Gretchen's aunt thought him to be a bad man. He claimed that he had spent quite a bit of money on Gretchen. Frances was concerned about his behavior during his second stay with her, describing him as acting like a madman. She mentioned that several of her other boarders had remarked on his behavior as well. In her opinion, Greiner was not in any state of mind to know right from wrong on the morning of the shooting. The defense asked her about some letters that had been written between Gretchen and Greiner in early August. They wanted to enter them into evidence, as they believed they would show a close relationship between the two. Frances said that a reporter had taken them on the day of the murder.

A short recess was called to allow Dr. Fitch of the Central Asylum for the Insane to examine Greiner in private. This was followed by another line of witnesses, who testified that Greiner and Gretchen had been courting in the year leading up to the murder. Dr. Fitch was then called to give his assessment of Greiner's mental health. He admitted that Greiner was hard to evaluate, as he refused to say much. Even so, his conclusion was that Greiner was "a man of low moral qualities and of impulses, and a subject of his passions."[78] He agreed with the defense that Greiner was "subject to insane delusions" and was medically insane when he killed Gretchen.[79] He clarified that the act of killing a woman for turning down a marriage proposal in itself was only evidence of low morality—not necessarily insanity. Greiner's other behaviors were the basis for the diagnosis of insanity.

Dr. Finch had been assisted by Dr. R. Wirth and Dr. J.L. Stillman in examining Greiner. Dr. Wirth was the next person to take the stand. He had examined Greiner while he was in jail and on the day before the trial started. In their first encounter, he found Greiner to be amiable but with no mental issues aside from nervousness. During the second examination, he noticed a scar on Greiner's head. Greiner said that he had received it while he was in Germany and that he had been in a hospital for three months because of it. This time, he noticed that Greiner seemed dull-witted and unable to comprehend simple questions. This indicated that he had some impairment of the nervous system. He saw no other symptoms that would lead him to consider Greiner insane. This led to a discussion of "emotional insanity," which Dr. Wirth explained as a man's emotions not being controlled by his will while being otherwise sane.[80] He found it plausible that Greiner could have been in this state when he killed Gretchen. He refused to opine on whether Greiner was legally insane but explained that being mentally unbalanced did not mean a man could not know right from wrong.

Yet another doctor, Dr. Erwin Heyl, had known Greiner for two years, as he had treated him for an injury at a previous job. He had more recently seen Greiner twice while he was in jail. Greiner had admitted a "secret vice" to him, which Dr. Heyl thought affected his sanity over the years.[81] This was a matter of great interest to the jury, who questioned Dr. Heyl about the degree of insanity this vice might cause. When presented with a series of hypothetical questions by the defense, Dr. Heyl was inclined to agree that Greiner had been medically insane. He conversely agreed with the prosecution that, without knowing the full facts of Greiner's case, Greiner's actions in the day or two surrounding the murder did appear to be those of a sane man.

Two more doctors were questioned about Greiner's sanity. Dr. J.L. Stillman, an assistant physician at the Columbus Hospital for the Insane, had mostly been acquainted with the case through the newspaper coverage of it. He had examined Greiner twice during the week. He characterized Greiner as insane, having a case of melancholia with delirium. Dr. Van S. Seltzer had treated Greiner for mental issues, including memory loss, for six months in 1883. He suspected that Greiner had a "vile habit," but his attempt to treat him for it did not work.[82] He noted that Greiner was obsessed with marriage. Greiner was concerned that if he did not get better, he could not marry. After months of hearing Greiner complain about his treatments, Dr. Seltzer told him to find another doctor. He believed that Greiner's actions around the day of the murder were those of a man "insane on love."[83] At the same time, he concurred with the prosecution that Greiner's actions were premeditated.

A second parade of witnesses, mostly Greiner's employers and coworkers, were brought in by the defense to describe his demeanor and habits at work. Again, they described him as hot-tempered. The general consensus was that Greiner was disorganized and showed either a lack of concern or incompetence in his work. One coworker found it odd that it was hard to catch Greiner's eye when speaking with him. They had no strong feelings about whether he seemed insane.

After the defense rested its case, the prosecution called a dozen or so additional doctors who had examined Greiner and other long-term acquaintances to weigh in on the question of his sanity. As expected of witnesses for the prosecution, their conclusion was that Greiner knew right from wrong when he pulled the trigger. Dr. Frank Warner, who worked with the mentally ill at the Ohio Penitentiary, added the disturbing detail that Greiner had confessed to have killed Gretchen to show her that no other man could have her.

Greiner was found guilty of murder in the first degree. The jury had needed only one vote to reach a unanimous decision. His execution date was set for July 24. Before passing his sentence, the judge asked Greiner if there was any reason why he should not be executed for the crime. Greiner's only response was a request to go to Green Lawn Cemetery to visit Gretchen's grave. Greiner appeared more distressed at Judge Wylie's refusal to let him see the grave than he was by the thought of his impending hanging.

Greiner's defense lawyer, E.T. DeLaney, filed a motion for a new trial, and he alleged jury tampering. The major basis for this was that the *Daily Times* had recently published an article ridiculing the notion of the insanity defense. Copies of that paper with the article marked had been sent to some of the jurors. Another issue was that the Deputy Sheriff William Heinmiller had discussed Greiner's behavior in jail with one of the jurors. Heinmiller admitted that he had discussed the case at his office but had not known at the time that one of the men there was on the jury. Judge Wylie went through the objections point by point with the defense, explaining why he did not think there was sufficient proof of their allegations.

Sheriff Heinmiller requested that Greiner be put under twenty-four-hour watch.

Almost a month after Greiner's sentencing, *The Columbus Evening Dispatch* brought up allegations that Judge Wylie was an alcoholic who had no business being on the bench. It pointed to a recent altercation in a saloon between Wylie and a German lawyer. The lawyer berated Wylie for appointing attorneys who spoke no German to defend Greiner, knowing that the defendant spoke little English. The lawyer was also upset that instead of saying "and may God have mercy on your soul" after pronouncing the death sentence, Wylie cursed him to hell.[84] The paper reported that Judge Wylie had been caught in previous drunken public escapades. A petition was being circulated to ask for his resignation.

More controversy played into the Greiner case when a dispute arose over whether his execution would be subject to a new law that required prisoners to be executed on the grounds of the Ohio Penitentiary instead of by the county as had traditionally been done. The state of Ohio had been averaging twenty-four executions a year throughout its eighty-eight counties. An amendment had been made to the new bill, clarifying that it would apply to cases in which the execution was set for July 1 and later—but not those prior to that date. Lieutenant Governor Warwick said that it would apply to Greiner and another prisoner who was sentenced to die in early July. The crux of the dispute was over whether the general assembly had the right to override the courts on any aspect of sentencing, including the place of execution. The amendment had been made to ensure that Valentine Wagner, who was scheduled to be executed on July 30, was hanged at the penitentiary. Penitentiary officials had also asked for a delay to give them time to erect a permanent building for the gallows. The new law required that the condemned be brought to the penitentiary thirty days before their execution.

Sheriff Heinmiller announced that unless the court officially changed the place of execution, he intended to hang Greiner in the county jail. He believed that to do otherwise would be in violation of court orders. Former prosecuting attorney W.J. Clarke explained that there was no legal precedent to move the place of execution after the sentence had been given. He suggested that the dilemma could be solved by moving Greiner to the penitentiary in accordance with the new law and then having that challenged in court. Governor George Hoadly threw in his two cents' worth and stated that he had no authority to change the place of execution, despite being able to grant clemency for the crime itself. He agreed with Clarke that it was a matter for the supreme court to address. Attorney General James Lawrence confirmed that since Greiner had been sentenced before the law was enacted, his sentence should not be affected by it.

In mid-June, Bertie Greiner received a troubling letter from her brother. In it, he asked her to bring him a revolver so that he could kill Sheriff Heinmiller and himself. He went on to say that if she could not do that, he wanted her to bring poison for him to commit suicide with. She notified the sheriff about the letter. He figured that it must have been smuggled out, as he inspected all outgoing letters from the prisoners. Greiner followed that letter with another, asking to be buried in the same manner as his victim. He grumbled that his trial was not fair and that wished those involved would get their just deserts. It was reported that whenever Bertie did go to the jail to visit her brother, he was thoroughly abusive to her. But this did not dissuade her renewed loyalty to him. She made a fruitless plea to Governor Hoadly to give him a stay of execution. In case the worst did come to pass, she saved money so that he could be buried next to Gretchen in Green Lawn Cemetery.

As the gallows were being built in the courthouse yard for Greiner's execution, his attorneys went before the circuit court to see if they could

Green Lawn Cemetery. *Courtesy of the Columbus Metropolitan Library.*

have the results of his trial overturned. Greiner's attorney Owen T. Gunning also appealed to Governor Hoadly to see if his sentence could be commuted to life in prison. In both cases, the requests were made on the basis of alleged errors made by the court of common pleas in its ruling and on claims of Greiner suffering from insanity. Hoadly replied that this was a matter for the supreme court. Gunning argued that the supreme court would not consider the case until the circuit court had decided on the appeal. Governor Hoadly agreed to grant a respite if this happened.

The county's attempt to build proper gallows was awkward. Sheriff Heinmiller had a special rope brought down from Cleveland for the noose. When he tested it on a 180-pound bag of sand, it broke.

Meanwhile, in his cell, Greiner spent his time with Reverend C.H. Rohe, who made daily visits, and reading a German Bible. He then seemed repentant, expressing sorrow for his crime and wanting the forgiveness of those he had wronged. He had a piece of twine that had knots made in it for every day he had left before his execution date. Every morning, he would remove one knot, watching the line of knots shorten just as his life was. He did enjoy the extra food and delicacies that were provided as a kindness for the condemned. *The Columbus Evening Dispatch* remarked on his growing girth. He was not pleased when a tailor from Lazarus Brothers was sent to measure him for a new suit for his execution. His days were also punctuated with visitors to the prison—mostly women—who came to gawk at him from behind the iron-barred door and cage that led to the cell room.

With only three days left before his execution date, Attorney Owen T. Gunning made an attempt to get a stay of execution from the Ohio Supreme Court. This proved to be a challenge. Only two of the judges were supposed to be in Columbus at the time. One of them, Judge Okey, was ill and could not receive him. The other, Judge Owen, had left the city to spend time in the forests of Michigan. Thus thwarted, Gunning sent letters to the homes of the remaining judges. Judge McIlvaine was out and never received the letter. Judges Johnson and Follett believed that the supreme court had no jurisdiction until the circuit court had made its decision. This would be too late to help Greiner. The circuit court had announced that it would not be making a decision until September.

Under the circumstances, Governor Hoadly finally broke down the following day and granted a stay of execution until October 17. He noted that his decision had no bearing on whether Greiner would be hanged at the county jail or in the penitentiary.

Not wanting the gallows to go to waste, Heinmiller and Deputy Albert Noethlith staged a mock execution for photographers. Heinmiller placed a hood over Noethlith's head, tied his hands behind his back and adjusted a noose around his neck. Noethlith became so unnerved by the seeming reality of the presentation that he fainted.

The long wait for decisions by the higher courts did not change the ultimate result. The circuit court turned down the appeal. The supreme court agreed with its decision and refused to overrule it. Greiner was despondent and put on a death watch. He was not too despondent to forgo having photographs taken of himself to give out as a final memento to his friends. His attorneys and his sister both made last-ditch attempts to get Hoadly to commute his sentence, emphasizing his alleged insanity. Governor Hoadly denied the appeal, saying, "The case is so clear that I have reached this decision without hesitation or doubt."[85]

When the morning of Greiner's doom finally arrived, the jail was thronged with would-be spectators. Out of respect for the gravity of the occasion, Sheriff Heinmiller had all view of the gallows blocked off from outside the jail. Even the prisoners in the jail were moved to cells out of sight of the gallows.

Greiner had spent his last night in fairly good spirits, receiving visitors who wished to say their farewells. He made a tearful goodbye to his sister, fretting that she would then need to go back to Germany. When asked about the murder, he continued to deny that Gretchen had refused to marry him. Wanting to eke the most out of every last minute he had, Greiner refused to go to bed until 1:00 a.m. He was up again at 6:00 a.m.

Wearing his new suit with a small bouquet of flowers pinned to the lapel, Greiner left his cell with a relaxed smile on his face. He made a last request of Dr. Obetz, "Be sure I am dead before you bury me."[86] He requested that a knife be plunged into his chest just to make sure. While making last-minute amends, Greiner asked Sheriff Heinmiller to forgive him for setting fire to the jail a few weeks earlier. He had hoped the jailers would open the doors, giving him a chance to escape.

As the hour of execution neared, the officials tested the gallows to make sure the new rope would hold up and that the machinery was functioning perfectly. The officials gave Greiner a cigar and his final meal—he was understandably too nervous to eat much. At 11:00 a.m., the invited witnesses were let in. A long table was set up for the newspapermen, and an area for spectators was located in the back. Greiner was brought out, still smoking his cigar. From the scaffold, he addressed the witnesses, saying, "Well, gentlemen, I am very soon to leave you. May God's blessing be on you all. I bid you all goodbye. That is all I have to say."[87]

It took another ten minutes for the lawmen to bind Greiner's arms and legs and double-check that the rope was the right length to kill him quickly. They put the noose around his neck and the hood over his face. Then they sprung the trapdoor. Eleven minutes later, Greiner was dead. For a few hours, his body was put on view at the Schoedinger Funeral Parlor, where the hundreds of curious onlookers from outside the jail got their chance to view the murderer. Then his body was moved to Green Lawn Cemetery. In the end, Gretchen got her wish to escape him. Instead of being buried next to her as he had asked, Greiner was buried at the far edge of the cemetery, well away from her.

10

THE RIVALS

E very community has its criminal element. No matter how law-abiding the majority of its citizens are, there will always be some who are law breakers—that is to be expected. What isn't expected is that trouble makes its way in from other cities. This was the case on April 19, 1913, when the small, mostly peaceable Chinese community in Columbus was rocked yet again, this time by a horrific attack involving two outsiders.

Motorcycle Officer Shaw was called just after 6:00 a.m. to a room at 266½ North Third Street in an area favored by the local Chinese population. He had been summoned there by Yee Jack, a former grocer in the area. There, Shaw found S.W. Tang, a Chinese interpreter from Baltimore, Maryland, lying dead on his bed with two bullet holes in his right temple. It appeared that he had been shot in his sleep. Another man, Woo Gew, lay nearby. He had an icepick in his head that had been driven through his skull with a hammer. Deep cut marks from a hatchet were scattered across his head, neck, abdomen and fingers. Miraculously, the elderly laundryman was still alive. He was rushed to St. Francis Hospital.

Yee Jack was held for questioning. He had been in the room with the other men at the time of the attacks but was not injured. He told police that Moy Fat, a twenty-year-old native of China, had committed the deeds. Police telegraphed all large cities and Ohio towns to alert them to be on the lookout for the suspect. As a Washington, D.C. resident, Moy Fat was unlikely to be hiding out in Columbus. Indications were that he had headed toward Springfield or Dayton.

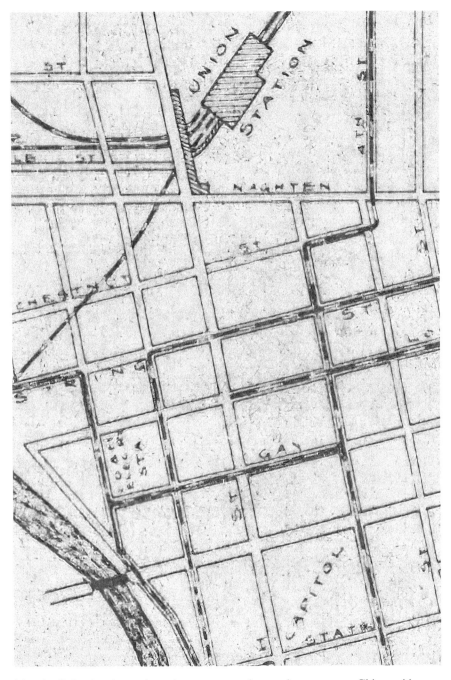

Map detail showing the northern downtown area that was home to many Chinese citizens in Columbus. *Courtesy of Columbus Metropolitan Library.*

The police believed that the murder was related to a war between Chinese tongs. The tongs were Chinese fraternal organizations or secret societies frequently associated with gang warfare. They surmised that S.W. Tang had been murdered for failing to obey an order from a tong. Tang was in Columbus to act as an official interpreter in a United States court case against Ng You Nuey, who was up for possible deportation. The victim had been warned to leave Columbus several weeks before.

Moy Fat turned out to be a fellow interpreter who worked privately. Police added the possibility that a personal rivalry may have been the motive. Another potential motive emerged regarding Yee Jack, the lone unharmed witness. He had recently sold his Chinese grocery but had not yet received full payment for it from Charles Ying, the new owner. The police considered that Yee Jack could have hired someone to maim or kill the men to expedite the business matter. It was unclear why they believed Tang or Woo Gew may have been involved in the sale.

When the police were able to procure another interpreter, Yee Jack gave his account of the morning's events. He shared a third-floor room on the corner of Chestnut and North Third Streets with Woo Gew and Tang. They were all asleep when Yee Jack was awakened by the sound of someone talking. He looked up to see a man with a hatchet hacking away at Woo Gew as he lay in his bed at the far end of the room. The attacker then took an ice pick and drove it into his victim's head with a hammer. Next, he walked over to Tang's bed and shot him twice before leaving the room. Yee Jack drew a diagram of the room for Sergeant of Detectives Dorgan, indicating the assailant's movements throughout the attack. Police found the icepick and pistol in a fireplace grate on the first floor.

By the end of the day, St. Francis Hospital had released the news that Woo Gew remained conscious and seemed to be regaining his strength. After a poor prognosis when he was first brought there, they then had hope that he might recover. By the next day, he was able to tell his version of events. His story corroborated the one told by Yee Jack. Yee Jack was released on a $1,000 bond.

As the investigation unfolded, the police were able to trace Moy Fat's movements after the murder. He walked south on Third Street to Rich Street, hoping to catch a trolley. Since there were none running in the area that early in the morning, he went to a taxicab company on that corner to hire a driver. He had the driver take him to Newark—thirty-five miles away—to drop him off at a laundry. The trip cost fifteen dollars, a hefty sum back then. The chauffeur found out on his return that his affluent fare was wanted for murder.

The police interviewed Der Doo, the head of the Baltimore Chinese community, to get his insight on the case. He agreed that Tang was likely killed by Moy Fat, who was acting as an agent for a tong, to keep him from testifying against the tong in a federal case. Violent tong activity was not unheard of in Ohio. Eighteen months earlier, Woo Dip, a Chinese man in Cleveland, narrowly escaped an assassination attempt by members of the Hip Sing Tong. Those tong members, who had fired three bullets at Woo Dip at close range, were then serving time in the Ohio Penitentiary.

Tang's background turned out to be more illustrious and varied than anyone would have guessed. His early life seemed like something out of an adventure novel. The Madagascar-born man was the son of C.P. Tang, a wealthy Chinese navy admiral. He had come to the United States when he was fourteen. Tang was well educated, having studied in London and at Columbia University. He went on to take a job with the Federal Bureau of Immigration in Baltimore as a secret serviceman. He worked for the bureau for several years, running down smugglers, opium dealers and illegal aliens. In between those assignments, Tang had a job on the side as a public speaker. He became well known for his illustrated lectures on China.

Tiring of government work, Tang settled in Cleveland and opened a Chinese restaurant. For a while, he also acted as the business agent and interpreter for the On Leong Tong in Cleveland. This made him highly regarded in the national organization. Unfortunately, he was a better interpreter than restaurateur. His restaurant in Cleveland failed, as did his effort to establish a café in the city's downtown area. In order to regain financial stability, he was forced to join the Hip Sing Tong. This did not sit well with the On Leong Tong, of which Moy Fat was also a prominent member. Tang received death threats that ordered him to leave Ohio.

Tang returned to Baltimore to work as an interpreter, this time as a private consultant. This went well. He soon gained a national reputation for his skill in that area. His latest trip to Columbus had kept him busy with jobs. Earlier in the week, Tang had acted as an interpreter in the court case of Frank Lee, a Chinese laundryman. That case involved the defendant pointing a gun at a North Side youth. Tang had impressed the court with his cosmopolitan manner of dress and intelligent demeanor.

The possible involvement of the tongs in the murder was a sensitive matter among other Chinese. They understandably did not want their community's reputation connected with organized crime. Gin Gun, a New York City interpreter who was working for the district attorney there, came to arrange the bond to release Yee Jack. Gin Gun hypothesized that someone had held a grudge against Tang for some testimony he had given in his work as an interpreter. He denied any knowledge of trouble with the tongs that may have led to the murder.

With Moy Fat still missing, Detective Bernard Bergin officially charged him with first-degree murder on April 22.

After a long bout of freedom, Moy Fat's luck ran out on October 1, when he was captured by the police in Philadelphia's Chinatown. Police and prosecutors of both cities worked together to determine if the eyewitnesses against Fat would need to go to Philadelphia to identify him. Detective Bernard Bergin, United States Inspector Oldfield and Assistant Prosecutor Ballard set off for Philadelphia to bring Moy Fat back to Columbus. In lieu of Yee Jack's and Woo Gew's testimony, the chauffeur who drove Moy Fat to Newark was brought along to identify him. The identification was positive.

Plans to prosecute Moy Fat were derailed when the witnesses to the murder, Woo Gew and Yee Jack, went missing. They had moved to Cleveland shortly after the murder but had since disappeared. Sergeant of Detectives John Dorgan expressed concern that they may have been spirited out of the country.

A hearing was held in Harrisburg, Pennsylvania, to determine if Moy Fat could be extradited to Columbus. The extradition hearing was muddied by testimonies that contradicted each other as well as the known specifics of the case. The reporting on the case further confused matters, as reporters mixed up April 18 and 19 and meshed the two witnesses to the murder, Yee Jack and Woo Gew, into one person. Two witnesses, Will Gray Beach and Dr. Anthony C. Neary, proclaimed that they had seen Moy at the federal building in Philadelphia on April 18. Two others, post office inspector J.F. Oldfield and Charles Alexander, testified that they had seen Moy Fat in Columbus on not only April 18 but also the following day.

Governor Tener of Pennsylvania agreed to extradite Moy Fat in spite of the lack of clarity in the matter. He was convinced by the attorney general there to let a jury decide who was telling the truth in the case of the conflicting witness testimonies.

A little over two weeks after his capture, Moy Fat, who sometimes went by the alias Henry Moy, was brought back to Columbus. Because he was charged with a capital crime, the state was allowed to keep him without bond until Yee Jack and Woo Gew were found. Detective Bergin, with the help of Philadelphia police, brought Tang's wife, Florence, to identify Moy Fat as her husband's enemy.

Artist's rendering of Moy Fat.
Author's collection.

Almost nine months passed before Moy Fat was let out on $7,500 bail. The release was pending the reappearance of witness Yee Jack. Police did manage to find the other witness, Woo Gew, in Cleveland, but he was in serious condition. He died shortly after. Despite languishing in jail for many months, Moy Fat still managed to cut a swanky figure. At the time of his release, the newspapers gushed over his Prince Albert suit and debonair manner.

Yee Jack remained elusive. Finally, in 1921, the case against Moy Fat was dropped, given the small likelihood that the sole witness would ever be found.

Tang made the papers for a final time in early 1924 in an article involving his wife and one of his sons.[88] While Tang was working for the government in Baltimore, he met Florence Adkins, a private school student and the daughter of real estate dealer. They were brought together by their deeply religious natures. When Florence's parents strongly objected to the idea of them marrying, they eloped to Philadelphia. After Tang's death, his father talked Florence into bringing his grandsons Calvert and Linwood to be raised in China. Florence, then Florence Leonard Duff, had remarried in the interim but had been widowed a second time. Admiral Tang died in 1923, leaving his son's widow and Linwood as his heirs, Calvert presumably having preceded him in death. Florence returned to China to bring Linwood and their inheritance, worth over $26 million in today's money, back to the United States.

11

THE JAILBREAKER

June 7, 1905

The break-in seemed to be going smoothly. Frank Conrad and his accomplice had managed to ransack the majority of the rooms in Horace L. Chapman's mansion at 111 East Broad Street with a speed and efficiency that would make any skilled burglar proud. There was no rush as far as they were concerned, as the Chapmans had left to spend their summer in cooler climes. The house was empty and would remain that way for weeks. Little did the thieves know that the Chapmans had a state-of-the-art silent alarm system installed by the American District Telegraph Company (ADT) before they left. The alarm had been tripped the moment that they had pried the window open to get in. The mere nine minutes that had passed had been enough time for the police to get an alert from ADT and bring a wagonload of officers to the address. It was not going to end well.

The police had the place surrounded. A couple of the officers entered the house through the kitchen door, with the rest keeping watch outside. The police pushed a button on the ADT system that turned all the lights in the house on at once. Neighbors watched curiously from their windows as police moved from room to room. A sound drew their attention to a curtained window, where they could see the shadows of two men. The curtains flew open to reveal the burglars. The curtains closed just as quickly when the men noticed the police waiting for them outside. Two minutes later, they heard

Officer Daniel E. Davis yell, "Halt! Halt!"[89] Two shots rang out. After a slight pause, more shots were heard. Then pandemonium broke out. Patrolman Reed saw Conrad after he leapt into the yard and managed to capture him. The other thief escaped in the confusion.

The policemen's triumph in stopping the burglary was soon deflated when they realized that Officer Davis was severely wounded. He had bullet holes in his chest and stomach. Davis was so near death that, at first, they thought he was already gone. He died on the way to the hospital. Davis had been on the police force for six years. Before that, he had worked as a railroad engineer. During his time on the force, he had gained a reputation for being hardworking and fearless. The well-liked officer was known for taking chances with his own life in order to protect others. He left behind a wife and an adult son.

Back at the crime scene, Patrolman Reed dragged Conrad through the house, hoping that he would reveal where his partner might be hiding. The other officers scoured the house and neighborhood looking for the escaped man.

Conrad, a good-looking, well-dressed young man, kept a cool demeanor throughout. He calmly smoked a cigar as he discussed the night's events. He seemed almost amused by it, asking, "Am I a circus?"[90] Police were sure that he was the man that they and Officer Davis had chased from Governor Herrick's house after it had been broken into a few nights prior. They discovered a chisel in his pocket that matched the chisel marks on the windows of the Herrick house and other homes that had recently been burglarized. They also found the revolver that had been used to kill Officer Davis. Conrad claimed that it belonged to him but that it had been given to his companion before the shooting.

Conrad tripped up his claims of innocence in the shooting the next day when he was having his measurements and photograph taken for his Bertillon card. Bertillon officer Harry French caught him off guard with this question: "What kind of a gun did you shoot Officer Davis with?"[91] Conrad answered that he had used a .38-caliber Smith and Wesson, shooting Davis in the heart.

A couple of saloonkeepers and a lodging house operator identified Conrad as a man who had been hanging around their establishments with a companion in the few days before the shooting. Conrad had shown off his ability to juggle beer glasses to one of the saloonkeepers, saying that he had been a bartender in Canton. With that lead, the police contacted their counterparts in Canton. The Canton police revealed that Frank Conrad was well known to them and that his real name was Frank Castor. They had reports that he had been seen in the company of Mike Murray, also known as Mike McCarney, in Canton the previous week. While Castor had told police that his partner was named John Reed, Murray fit the description of the man he had been seen with in Columbus. Canton police announced that they had caught Murray and that they would be sending him back to Columbus. The man they arrested claimed that he could produce witnesses to attest that he had been in Cleveland the night of the killing. Two days later, reports came out that Murray was still on the loose. It turned out that the man that the police had been arrested as "Mike Murray" was Canton saloonkeeper James O'Neill.

Artist's rendering of Frank Castor, also known as Frank Conrad. *Author's collection.*

The police suspected that Conrad and Murray may have had a female accomplice. They based this on an incident that occurred shortly before the burglarizing of the home of Governor Myron T. Herrick. A well-dressed woman stopped Sergeant Harlow to ask some questions about the state hospital. She went on to ask him where Governor Herrick's home was, wanting to know its exact location. It had been reported in the papers that the Herricks were in New York, making the house an easy mark. Sergeant Harlow became suspicious. When he started questioning her in return, she was suddenly in a hurry to leave.

Castor already had a long record of criminal activity. Originally from Detroit, he spent time in the penitentiary in Jackson, Michigan. He escaped from the prison and fled to Cleveland. While there, he was shot in the leg during a saloon brawl. Then he moved on to Canton, where he was frequently seen with Murray.

More stories about Castor's illegal activities began pouring in from other cities and states. Police Officer E.E. Bishop of Saginaw, Michigan, confirmed that Castor was no stranger to violence. When he arrested Castor for burglary two years prior, Castor shot at him five times. Chief of Police E.I. Brady of Dunkirk, New York, believed that Castor was one of two men who were frightened off by servants while burglarizing a house there. The thieves dropped most of their loot, but they did manage to make off with two revolvers that matched the one that killed Detective Davis. Castor's description fit one of the men involved in the Dunkirk burglary, as well as a rash of recent burglaries in Akron.

Castor's criminal network turned out to be more extensive than anyone realized. He spent his time in the county jail writing to a pal in Canton, Peter Mathias, plotting a jailbreak. He asked Mathias to bring a package of explosives and a "rod" to a livery stable behind the jail.[92] From there, his friend George Hite was to slip the package to him in the jail. Hite thought better of it and cooperated with the police to thwart the plot.

Franklin County sheriff George Karb had set up a sting operation even before that. He had a Black trustee befriend Castor and earn his confidence. The trustee told Castor that he could smuggle letters out for him through another trustee. The second, fictitious trustee had privileges that allowed him to be outside of the jail. This would bypass the usual checks the inmates' outgoing mail went through. The trustee warned the killer that the letters could not be sealed, as his accomplice was afraid of potentially breaking federal laws regarding mail. Castor took the bait. As he sent out each letter through the trustee, the letter would be handed over to Karb. The originals were kept, while a copy was sent on to the intended recipient.

A letter to "Black Pete" Mathias dated August 15 proved that Karb's instincts were right. In it, Castor requested a half pint of "soup," the slang for nitroglycerine in the criminal underworld. Almost a week later, he sent another letter, and this one was more urgent. He was concerned that the grand jury would meet for his case soon. This time, he requested a gun in addition to the explosives. He warned Mathias to make the package as small as possible to make it easier to smuggle in.

Karb asked Will J. Koehl, whose livery barn was behind the jail, to let him know of any suspicious activity. After a week, Karb and Koehl hit pay dirt. A rough-looking man with a package under his arm came around asking for Hite. Koehl told him that Hite was away for a bit but should be back in an hour or two. The man said that he would be back in an hour. Koehl then informed Karb, who stationed deputies in the basement of the courthouse in sight of the stable. Karb kept watch from his office in the courthouse as well.

Around noon, Karb left the courthouse, only to happen upon the sight of the rough-looking man with a package under his arm on Mound Street, around the corner from the stable. As the man approached his destination, Hite asked if he was looking for someone. He said that he was looking for Hite. After they identified themselves to each other, Hite suggested that they hide the package in the hay in Koehl's barn for Hite to deliver later. The man felt that this was not private enough, so they agreed to hide it in Hite's own barn. Unknown to him, "Hite's" barn was actually the jail's barn.

Hite lifted his hat to scratch his head to signal to the deputies that the man with him was the right one. A man who had been standing by an automobile on Mound Street jumped in his car and took off when he saw Deputies E.L. Phelan, Joseph Klunk and County Jailer Reedy MacDonald hurriedly walk to the barn. In the interest of public safety, they chose to let the probable second conspirator drive away. Knowing that the package contained nitroglycerine, the deputies had to wait until it was safely set down. If the man holding the package heard a commotion and started running, it could be disastrous. Once Hite and the conspirator finished hiding the package, they headed off to a saloon for a drink. The deputies closed in.

Castor's friend put up a fight, but it came to a quick end when he attempted to pull a gun on McDonald—only to reach into the wrong pocket. McDonald took advantage of the gaffe to get his own revolver shoved up underneath the thug's chin. Ever the tough guy, the man groused, "You'se kin shoot if you wants to. I never went back on a friend, and I tink I will now. Just do what youse want, but there's nothin' coming from me."[93] While McDonald and Klunk escorted the man to the jail, Deputies Phelan and Connor went into the barn to retrieve the package. They walked on their tiptoes, handling the package gingerly with the knowledge that it was

Franklin County Jail. *Courtesy of the Columbus Metropolitan Library.*

highly explosive. When they opened it inside the jail, they found that it contained a dozen steel saws, fuses, cord, a revolver and a pint bottle that was swathed in cotton.

Professor Weber of the Ohio State University performed a chemical analysis of the bottled liquid. He confirmed that it was nitroglycerin. One test involved hitting a small drop of it with a hammer. That tiny amount was enough to create a small explosion as loud as a gunshot. The amount that was in the package was enough to blow a huge hole in the courthouse.

A letter enclosed in the package read:

August 25, 1905

Friend Frank: You now have everything you need. Kindly use this soup nitroglycerin sparingly. A teaspoonful or tablespoonful will do all you want in a tight place. Soap all cracks well, after putting in soup. Take strips of old blanket and soak with soup and put in cracks. Soap up afterwards or else take cotton, which you will find inside. A piece of fuse is shown here how to fix fuse with cap. Bite cap as shown, make cup this way [at this point in the note, a cup is drawn to illustrate the manner of fixing the fuse] *and press up against window or wherever you have space. Split end of fuse, so it will burn. It is a fast fuse.*

John O'Brien[94]

A letter from Castor that was found on the man indicated a friendly relationship between the two. He wrote of how he was faring in jail, with no mention of the proposed jailbreak.

Chief of Detectives James Dundon recognized their captive as a man he had seen in a Canton saloon while he was there searching for Murray. The police originally thought he was John O'Brien but later identified him as Jud King.

Back in Canton, Peter Mathias was charged with aiding and abetting a prisoner charged with felony to escape. They took extra caution with him on the way back to Columbus, as previously, a prisoner in transit had escaped by blowing cayenne pepper into the eyes of his captors. The caution was warranted, as they had already been met at the station by a crowd of criminals and warned to leave before nighttime to avoid any trouble. On the trip back, they took a roundabout route to sidestep potential trouble in Zanesville.

In order to keep Castor in the dark about the failed attempt to break him out of jail, King was kept isolated from other prisoners. There were some concerns that he might try to contact Castor through the "telegraph" system penitentiary inmates had developed by tapping on gas pipes. The police, likewise, placed Mathias in a different area of the jail. None of the men knew that the others, aside from Castor, had been jailed. The ruse worked. Castor sent out another letter to Mathias, worried that he had not received his package.

While King remained staunchly close-mouthed, Mathias chattily informed the police of whatever he could about Castor and his friends. He and Castor knew each other from their time working as bartenders at Tim O'Neill's saloon in Canton. He confirmed that Mike Murray had left Canton a day after Castor. Murray had claimed that he was heading for Cleveland. Mathias had not seen King for a couple of weeks but thought that he might be frequenting another Canton saloon. Despite being happy to spill the beans on the others, he denied having any knowledge of the plot to free Castor.

James "Tip" O'Neil was arraigned for taking part in the plot. He pleaded not guilty.

Castor found himself in even deeper trouble in early September. Chief of Police Frank H. Watson and County Detective Edward Wagner had been in pursuit of Castor for another burglary and cop killing in their city in May. The crime involved the theft of valuables and some high-end Brooks Brothers clothing. Near the home, they found the body of Police Detective Sergeant James Higgins with a coat from the burglary close by. The Erie detectives determined that Castor, who had been in their city at the time, was the likely suspect. They trailed him from state to state. When Castor was arrested in Columbus, he was wearing a coat with "Brooks Brothers" stamped on the buttons. The coat was sent back to Erie to be identified by the owner.

On September 3, the grand jury determined that Castor should be tried for first-degree murder. A couple of days earlier, Castor had figured out that his attempts to have his friend break him out of jail had failed. He went into a fury, smashing the furniture in his cell. Sheriff Karb had his suspicions that Castor was going to fake being insane to get out of the charges against him. The sheriff delayed punishing him until after the grand jury hearing. After that, Castor was moved to a cell in the "dungeon" of the jail and was to be given only water.

Castor's conspirators did not fare any better in their hearings with the grand jury. Peter Mathias, Jud King and James "Tip" O'Neil, a third member of the plot the police had later identified, were all indicted for attempting to break a felon out of the county jail. All three pleaded not guilty.

Karb's prediction about Castor appeared to be coming true. Dr. Hane reported that he had been suffering from nervous strain in the weeks following his hearing. Castor stayed in bed, eating little, and acted like he did not recognize anyone. Hane agreed that part of Castor's condition was being exaggerated for show but said that he truly was suffering from a nervous condition. The probate court appointed Dr. D.S. Deuschle and Dr. H.C. Rutter to make a series of examinations of Castor to determine his sanity. The "alienists," psychiatrists who specialized in the legal aspects of mental illness, decided to put him under constant watch for three days, thinking that he could not constantly fake being mentally undone for that amount of time. The jail physicians noted that he had previously feigned insanity for nine months to try to escape punishment while he was in the state reformatory.

The guards observed that Castor barely moved in his sleep. The then-current line of thought was that the mentally ill tossed and turned frequently in their sleep. After about a week, Castor changed tactics. Instead of being unresponsive, he became abusive toward his guards. Anticipating that he would become violent, the alienists had everything taken out of Castor's cell. Castor then relapsed into a catatonic state. The alienists were not impressed. They surmised that he had figured out how to put himself into a hypnotic state in order to feign insanity. They explained that being in the hypnotic state for extended periods of time interfered with his digestive system, leading to his disinterest in food. In turn, that led to his weakness. There were telltale signs that Castor was faking it. They noticed that when a piano could be heard playing from the street, Castor's foot would continually tap in time to the music.

By this point, Castor's arraignment had been pushed back for weeks while his mental health was being evaluated. It was decided that he would be arraigned whatever his condition. If he continued to be unresponsive at the arraignment, a plea of not guilty would automatically be entered for him. The arraignment on October 14 proved to be quite the spectacle. Castor, still feigning a nervous condition, was carried in on the shoulders of two brawny men. He twitched, puffed, rolled his eyes and ran his fingers through his hair while crouching at the bottom of his chair. He paid no attention to the proceedings. As previously announced, Judge Marcus G. Evans entered a plea of not guilty for him. Ulric Sloane, then acting as Castor's defense attorney, objected. He argued that more observation was needed to determine whether Castor should be put before a lunacy jury.

Judge Sloane decided that the assessment of the alienists was sufficient. Castor's trial was set for December 4.

When Sheriff Karb was asked if he had any plans to treat Castor for his silence, Karb smiled and indicated that he had something up his sleeve.

Sheriff George Karb, Castor's wily nemesis, was as likeable as Castor was dastardly. *The Columbus Evening Dispatch* described him as a "genial fellow" with a "kindly, cheerful disposition."[95] It touted, "He judges men, not by what they have, but what they are.…His application of the Golden Rule in his dealings with his fellows, whether in private or in public life, has been one of his chief characteristics."[96] A Columbus native, Karb had already had a varied career before becoming sheriff. He

George Karb. *Courtesy of the Columbus Metropolitan Library.*

had originally been a druggist, served on the city council, been mayor twice and had been a member of the police commission. He worked to clean up the city, both figuratively and literally. One of his goals as sheriff was to correct the unsanitary conditions in the jail, putting in a long overdue plumbing system.

Jud King was the first of the conspirators to be tried. It only took the jury ten minutes of deliberation to find him guilty. King's attorney, Judge Earnhart, filed a motion for a new trial. His contention was that King had been set up by Karb in the sting operation and that Castor had never received the explosives.

Judge Evans gave in to the demands of Castor's attorneys to have him further evaluated by other mental health specialists. The new team was Dr. George Stockton, the superintendent of the Columbus State Hospital, and alienist Dr. C.A. Howell. They tried to get the prisoner talking by dosing him up with ether. This only partially worked. He talked—but only in mumbles. Once the doctors announced that they would be reporting their findings, which indicated Castor was not mentally ill, he miraculously came out of his trance and began crying to see his relatives.

On the day his trial began, Castor withdrew his plea of not guilty and pleaded guilty. The jury was dismissed, although the trial continued for

Judge Evans to determine the degree of his guilt. It came out in the trial that Officer Davis had been shot outside of the house. There was speculation that the defense hoped to prove that the murder occurred after the robbery. This would free Castor from a state statute that required a death sentence when murder was committed during a robbery.

Castor told his life story when he took the stand. He was born in Flint, Michigan. Leaving home at the age of sixteen, he sought employment at the World Fair in Chicago. There, he worked in a livery and a university hotel. When those jobs ended, he took up with a peddler from New York. They traveled together throughout New York, Ohio and Indiana, selling novelties, for five years. He was arrested after burglarizing a home in Kalamazoo, Michigan, and was sentenced to four years at the Michigan State Reformatory. Castor testified that two convicts had committed the crime and were trying to put the blame on him, yet he pleaded guilty to get a lighter sentence.

After Castor was paroled, he joined his father in his house moving business. This lasted for a year and a half before a drinking spree landed Castor in trouble again. While in Saginaw, Michigan, he broke into a house, drunkenly believing it to be his home. He got into a gun battle with a policeman while trying to escape. This landed him in the Michigan State Penitentiary. The handsome young prisoner convinced a nurse to saw the bars off a window at the prison hospital where he was recuperating. They both escaped, avoiding capture.

While rambling around northern Ohio for several months, Castor was arrested a few times on minor charges. This is when he began working as a bartender at "Tip" O'Neill's saloon in Canton. Ever on the move, he headed to Columbus for work, making an unplanned stay in a Zanesville hospital after accidentally shooting himself in the ankle.

According to Castor, Columbus was where he met "Jack Reed." The two spent a few days hitting up the local saloons. While passing the Chapman house, Reed suggested, on a whim, that they burglarize the place. Castor's gun got caught on the windowsill as he was crawling in the window. He handed the gun to Reed, who kept playing with it. The gun was unloaded, but he knew that Reed was carrying bullets of various sizes. The shooting started when the crooks jumped off the roof to escape the police. Castor climbed a fence after the shots were fired, but he was soon caught.

Castor's lawyers argued for a lighter sentence on three counts. They said that the break-in was not a burglary because there was no evidence that anything was taken. If it was a burglary, the murder happened outside, after the burglary was finished. And if the murder did count as part of the burglary, it was not fair to hold Castor responsible for something Reed had allegedly done.

Judge Evans wasn't buying it. He found Castor guilty of first-degree murder. His reasoning was that the intent of the break-in was to burglarize. The defendant and his partner had been interrupted by the police and forced to flee. This was a different situation than it would have been if the men had chosen to leave empty-handed without provocation. Castor was within a few feet of Officer Davis when he was shot. There was no evidence that the other man had a gun, nor was he seen near Davis. Judge Evans stated that, given the grave penalty for the crime, he had tried in vain to find any evidence that would allow him to recommend mercy. When asked by Judge Evans, even Castor agreed that there was no reason he should not be sentenced to death. Castor himself was a believer in capital punishment. The death sentence was passed with orders to move Castor to the Ohio Penitentiary to await execution on April 6. Castor was remarkably calm about his sentence, even laughing about it. His attorneys vowed to appeal to higher courts—up to the United States Supreme Court if necessary.

Castor's would-be rescuers were being sorted through the courts. "Tip" O'Neil, whose trial was moved to Newark to avoid any prejudice in the jury, beat his charge. His jury did not believe the prosecution's claim that the letters from Castor addressed to the illiterate "Black Pete" Mathias were truly meant for O'Neil. O'Neil's acquittal weakened the case against Mathias—to the point that Prosecuting Attorney Karl T. Webber had the charge dropped. Mike Murray, Castor's accomplice the night of the burglary, was eventually caught at Niagara Falls in June 1908. By that point, there were no witnesses who could positively identify him, so the charges against him were also dropped.

Castor made the news again with the announcement that he would be converting to Catholicism. Never a man who had much use for religion, his impending death made him desire to adopt his Catholic mother's faith.

Throughout his imprisonment, Castor managed to maintain a cheerful disposition, confident that the higher courts would come through for him in time. But things were not looking as optimistic as he supposed. With two weeks left before his execution date, the circuit court ruled that Castor's death sentence should stand. Castor's sense of his impending doom was heightened by a series of tests that were done on the electric chair to ensure that it was functioning correctly. Regardless, Castor's optimism was not unwarranted. On April 3, 1906, the Ohio Supreme Court granted the motion to file a petition in error. That action suspended Castor's execution until the court had time to review and decide on the case in October.

The death annex at the penitentiary started filling up. By August, Castor had been joined by William Hammell, Dr. Oliver C. Haugh, Ben Dickerson and Butler Styles, all of whom had suspended sentences. The men complained of boredom and lack of exercise to the guards, who could not do much about their situation. Indeed, formerly active Castor had gotten quite pale and thin from his long confinement. There was little chance that Warden Gould would agree to let them out in the yard for some fresh air and exercise if they had asked. Three of the condemned followed in Castor's footsteps and developed an interest in the Catholic faith. The little cellblock became known as the most religious in the penitentiary.

October arrived, bringing unwelcome news for Castor. The Ohio Supreme Court upheld Judge Evans's decision to apply the death sentence to his case. The news did not shatter Castor's calm demeanor. He remained ever hopeful that Governor Andrew L. Harris would grant him a pardon. His new date of execution was set for November 23.

A delegation of officials and religious leaders from Castor's hometown of Flint, Michigan, petitioned Governor Harris to stay the execution. They were laboring under the mistaken belief that Castor had been illegally denied a trial by jury. Harris conceded and granted Castor a reprieve on his death sentence until January 25. The matter was then to go before the pardon board on November 22, and failing that, it would be taken to the United States Supreme Court.

In light of this decision, the Columbus police started a petition that was to be circulated to policemen statewide to keep his sentence intact. They cited Castor's "cold cruelty and brutality" and "long criminal record" as proof that Castor killed Davis "with cold deliberation."[97] They reasoned:

> *The man who will daringly enter a place equipped for his crime as Castor was, cares not for the lives of those who may oppose him. The innocent are compelled to suffer, and if such criminals understand that they will be forced only to pay the same penalty for the crime of burglary alone, if caught, they, at once, prefer to take the chance of gaining freedom by shooting and killing if necessary, the man who stands between them and the open world.*[98]

Reformatory officers in Michigan joined in the fight, sending a letter to Governor Harris reminding him of Castor's bad record in their state.

The matter went before the parole board in February. Prosecuting Attorney Webber echoed the sentiment of the police. He pointed out that commuting Castor's sentence would send a signal to criminals that the laws of Ohio were not to be feared. He reminded them that Castor had been connected to another police murder during a burglary attempt in Erie, Pennsylvania. The defense was still trying to pin the murder on Castor's accomplice and argued that Castor had no reason to anticipate that bringing a gun to the burglary might end with someone's death. The parole board unanimously decided against Castor. Once again, Governor Harris granted a stay of execution until February 15 to allow the matter to be brought before the United States Supreme Court.

Castor's attorneys dragged their feet on presenting the case to the United States Supreme Court. There was speculation that they were purposely trying to delay the presentation to push the execution date back further. A few days before the planned execution, there was no indication that they had contacted the federal court at all.

Castor lost his cockiness that he would be saved from execution. He protested bitterly to the newspapers that he had been railroaded but also announced that he was prepared to meet his death. In the hopes of gaining another respite, he started making confessions that were too vague to be of any use to the police in convicting his accomplices. Among his confessions was a list of places in Ohio that he had burgled, which he sent to Governor Harris. He requested to have his execution delayed another thirty days so that he could confess to all his crimes. Governor Harris was not swayed. The testing of the electric chair resumed.

The day before his execution, Frank Castor declared, "I'm going to fight the chair until the last minute."[99] He continued to work with police, discussing cases that he might have knowledge of while also continuing to provide no information of worth. He did bring up that he had spent time in the Iowa Reformatory, which the police had not previously been aware of.

Castor's nerves were fraying. He had barely eaten anything in the four days leading up to the execution date. In his final hour, he became quite ill from the combination of starvation, cigar smoking and stress. Noticeably frail, he managed to walk unassisted to the death chamber and sat down in the electric chair. At midnight on February 15, he was strapped into the chair. Castor began thanking people for their kindness and help, only for his voice to fade away midsentence. Once it became clear that he had no more to say, 1,750 volts of electricity were shot through his body twice. He was later buried in Mount Calvary Cemetery.

Castor's death that night did not end his story. Almost two years later, an odd tale came out of the county jail. Trustee Walter Keplie was seen running up the basement steps and collapsing in a dead faint. Jailer McDonald revived him. Keplie explained that he had gone into the jail's basement to check on a fire in the range. A cold blast of air hit his face and blew out his lantern. He felt something approach him and then heard, "I am the spirit of Frank Castor, and I am going to kill you."[100]

NOTES

1. The Gangsters

1. "Detective Cline Dies After Hilltop Bank Thugs Are Slain," *Columbus Evening Dispatch*, February 5, 1938, 2.
2. "Bandit Hoped to Kill Gang Member," *Columbus Evening Dispatch*, February 5, 1938, 2.
3. "Stephen Figuli, Sucker," *Columbus Sunday Dispatch*, February 5, 1938, 4.
4. "Bandit Declared He Had Hoped to Kill Gang Member," *Columbus Evening Dispatch*, February 5, 1938, 1.
5. "Bandit Hoped," *Columbus Evening Dispatch*, 2.
6. "Bragging Bandit Says He Is Sorry," *Columbus Evening Dispatch*, February 5, 1938, 2.
7. "Bragging Bandit Sorry He 'Plugged' Detective," *Columbus Evening Dispatch*, February 5, 1938, 1.
8. "Bragging Bandit Says," *Columbus Evening Dispatch*, 2.
9. Ibid.
10. Ohio Department of Health, death certificate 9146, 1938, Unidentified White Man, Ohio History Connection, Columbus, OH.
11. "Figuli Trial Will Go to Jury Today," *Columbus Evening Dispatch*, March 10, 1938, 10.
12. "Governor Refuses Figuli's Appeal to Escape Chair," *Columbus Evening Dispatch*, December 20, 1938, 1.

13. "Figuli Calm as He Goes to Death," *Columbus Evening Dispatch*, December 22, 1938, 1.
14. Ibid., 6.

2. The Body in the Well

15. "Murder Will Out: The Ginniver Mystery at Last Explained," *Columbus Evening Dispatch*, February 4, 1889, 4.
16. Ibid.
17. Ibid.
18. Ibid.
19. "The Jury Is Impanneled," *Columbus Evening Dispatch*, July 2, 1889, 4.
20. "Ginever and the Soldiers," *Columbus Evening Dispatch*, December 10, 1889, 4.

3. The Christmas Eve Cop Killer

21. "Patrolman Is Murdered by a Drunken Youth," *Columbus Evening Dispatch*, December 25, 1908, 1.

4. The Legacies of Murder

22. "Detectives Still Lack 'Good Leads' in Two Slayings," *Columbus Evening Dispatch*, April 11, 1948, 7.
23. "Clues Lacking, Victims Found Stabbed to Death in Hotel, Residence," *Columbus Evening Dispatch*, April 1, 1948, 4.
24. "Leads Exhausted in Knife Murders of Two Women," *Columbus Evening Dispatch*, April 3, 1948, 1.
25. "Suspect Is Held in Investigation of 18th St. Murder," *Columbus Evening Dispatch*, April 4, 1948, 32.
26. "Witnesses Fail to Pick Suspect," *Columbus Evening Dispatch*, April 9, 1948, 2.
27. "Detectives Still Lack," *Columbus Evening Dispatch*, 7.
28. "Woman Sought as Slayer of Mona McBride," *Columbus Evening Dispatch*, July 16, 1948, 1.
29. Ibid.

30. Ibid.

31. Ibid.

32. "Youth Confesses 18th St. Murder," *Columbus Evening Dispatch*, January 15, 1949, 3.

33. Ibid.

34. "Sleuths Seeking Slayer of Women," *Columbus Evening Dispatch*, February 20, 1949, 54.

35. "Man Says He 'Probably' Killed Woman in Hotel," *Columbus Evening Dispatch*, February 22, 1949, 1.

36. Ibid.

37. "Ask Release of Smilack," *Columbus Evening Dispatch*, June 4, 1952, 1.

38. ACLU of Ohio, "*State Ex Rel. Smilack v. Bushong 159 Ohio St. 259.*"

39. Ibid.

40. "Youth Hopes to Reform, Talks Way to Pen to Study Bible," *Columbus Evening Dispatch*, June 18, 1954, 3.

5. The Chinese Question

41. "Personal," *Columbus Evening Dispatch*, August 26, 1881, 4.

42. "Capital Notes," *Cleveland Leader*, 2.

43. "A Chinese Mystery," *Columbus Evening Dispatch*, August 28, 1886, 4.

44. "Celestial Woes," *Columbus Evening Dispatch*, November 29, 1898, 8.

6. The Other One-Armed Man

45. "Salesman Sought in Slaying Here," *Columbus Evening Dispatch*, April 26, 1951, 4.

46. "Sticks to Story of Telephone Talk," *Columbus Evening Dispatch*, April 30, 1951, 4.

47. "Hair Clue in Alter Death 'Unwanted.' Pathologist Says," *Columbus Evening Dispatch*, May 8, 1951, 1.

48. "Alter to Conduct Own Investigation," *Columbus Evening Dispatch*, May 1, 1951, 1.

49. "Friends and Relatives Can't Believe Accusations Against Phillips," *Columbus Evening Dispatch*, May 19, 1951, 1.

50. Ibid.

51. Ibid.

52. "Man Charged as Alter Slayer Pleads Innocent," *Columbus Evening Dispatch*, May 19, 1951, 1.
53. "Here's Police Theory of What Happened," *Columbus Evening Dispatch*, May 20, 1951, 1.
54. "Cabbie Says He Took Man Resembling Alter to Death Scene," *Columbus Evening Dispatch*, October 31, 1951, 2.
55. "Says Phillips Once Wavered," *Columbus Evening Dispatch*, October 26, 1951, 1.
56. "State, Defense Rest; Jury Gets Phillips Murder Case Friday," *Columbus Evening Dispatch*, November 8, 1951, 17.
57. "Did Not Murder Ruth Alter, George Phillips Tells Jury," *Columbus Evening Dispatch*, November 3, 1951, 3.

7. The Red Shoe Mystery

58. "No Trace Found of Missing Girl," *Columbus Evening Dispatch*, February 26, 1946, 6.
59. Ibid.
60. "Motorist Sought in Celli Mystery," *Columbus Evening Dispatch*, February 28, 1946, 6.
61. "Eight Years of Waiting, Lola Celli's Family Still Hopeful Missing Daughter Will Be Found," *Columbus Sunday Dispatch*, February 21, 1954, 143.
62. "Check Tip that Missing Celli Girl Is Working in Virginia," *Columbus Evening Dispatch*, June 3, 1955, 23.

8. The Downward Spiral

63. "Unknown Young Woman Found Murdered in Deshler Hotel Room; Clothing Bore Trademarks of Columbus Merchants," *Columbus Evening Dispatch*, January 12, 1917, 1.
64. "First-Degree Murder Charge Against Wells," *Columbus Evening Dispatch*, January 13, 1917, 2.
65. Ibid.
66. "Mona Simon, Country Girl, Whom Lights of City Lured to Destruction and Death," *Columbus Evening Dispatch*, January 13, 1917, 3.
67. Ibid.

68. "Says Son Insane," *Columbus Sunday Dispatch*, January 14, 1917, 2.
69. "Let Us Think of Nobler Things," *Columbus Sunday Dispatch*, May 14, 1917, 4.
70. "Technical Plea of Not Guilty Made by Wells," *Columbus Evening Dispatch*, January 15, 1917, 3.
71. Ibid.
72. Ibid.

9. The Spurned Suitor

73. "Murder Number Two, A Discarded Lover Shoots His Sweetheart This Morning," *Columbus Evening Dispatch*, September 5, 1884, 1.
74. "The Seeling Murder," *Columbus Evening Dispatch*, September 6, 1884, 4.
75. "The Greiner Murder Trial," *Columbus Evening Dispatch*, March 16, 1885, 4.
76. Ibid.
77. Ibid., 2.
78. "Testimony for the Defense," *Columbus Evening Dispatch*, March 18, 1885, 4.
79. Ibid.
80. "Testing His Sanity," *Columbus Evening Dispatch*, March 19, 1885, 3.
81. "A Question of Insanity," *Columbus Evening Dispatch*, March 19, 1885, 4.
82. Ibid.
83. Ibid.
84. *Columbus Evening Dispatch*, April 25, 1885, 2.
85. "His Doom Sealed," *Columbus Evening Dispatch*, October 16, 1885, 4.
86. "Dropped into Eternity," *Columbus Evening Dispatch*, October 17, 1885, 4.
87. Ibid.

10. The Rivals

88. "Chinese Tragedy Recalled by Widow's Impending Return," *Columbus Evening Dispatch*, January 21, 1924, 3.

11. The Jailbreaker

89. "Is Shot to Death by a Desperate Burglar," *Columbus Evening Dispatch*, June 8, 1905, 2.

90. Ibid.

91. Ibid.

92. "Last Letter Written by Murderer Frank Castor to His Pal, Urging Assistance to Escape," *Columbus Sunday Dispatch*, August 27, 1905, 1.

93. "Desperados Lay Plot to Blow Up the County Jail," *Columbus Sunday Dispatch*, August 27, 1905, 7.

94. "Details of the Capture," *Columbus Sunday Dispatch*, August 27, 1905, 7.

95. "Bearding the Sheriff in His Den," *Columbus Sunday Dispatch*, October 22, 1905, 10.

96. Ibid.

97. "Police Believe Castor Should Suffer as the Courts Decreed," *Columbus Evening Dispatch*, November 14, 1906, 1.

98. Ibid.

99. "I'm Going to Fight the Chair Until the Last Minute—Frank Castor," *Columbus Evening Dispatch*, February 14, 1907, 1.

100. "Ghost of Castor Threatened Him," *Columbus Sunday Dispatch*, December 27, 1908, 2.

BIBLIOGRAPHY

ACLU of Ohio. "*State Ex Rel. Smilack v. Bushong 159 Ohio St. 259* (Ohio 1953)." April 22, 1953. www.acluohio.org.

The City of Columbus: The Capital of Ohio and the Great Railway Center of the State. Columbus, OH: Columbus Board of Trade, 1885.

Cleveland Leader. "Capital Notes." May 20, 1884, 2.

Columbus City Prison, Lazarus Historical Photo Collection.

"Columbus Crime Scrapbook 1932–1940." Columbus Metropolitan Library, Columbus, Ohio.

Columbus Evening Dispatch. Various articles.

Columbus Illustrated. Columbus, OH: International Publishing Company, 1889.

Columbus Sunday Dispatch. Various articles.

County Jail, Columbus, OH. New York: A.C. Bosselman and Company, 1909.

FamilySearch. "New York Passenger Lists, 1820–1891. Sarah J. Ginever, 1882; citing Immigration, New York City, New York, United States, NARA microfilm publication M237 (Washington, D.C.: National Archives and Records Administration, n.d.), FHL microfilm 1,027,018." www.familysearch.org.

Franklin County at the Beginning of the Twentieth Century. Columbus, OH: Historical Publishing Company, 1901.

Franklin County Ohio Probate Court, declaration of intention, 1892, Phillip Sauter. Vol. 4, 184. Ohio History Connection, Columbus.

Harvey, T. Edgar, and the United Commercial Travelers of America. *Commercial History of the State of Ohio* no. 1. 1916.

Map of Columbus and Vicinity 1946. Columbus, OH: City of Columbus, 1946.

Modie & Kilmer's Folio Atlas of Franklin County. Columbus, OH: Modie and Kilmer, 1910.

Nast, Thomas. "The Chinese Question." *Harper's Weekly*, February 18, 1871, 149.

Ohio Department of Health. Death certificate 1570, 1926, Phillip Sauter. Ohio History Connection. Columbus, OH.

———. Death certificate 23241, 1948, Etta Marian Ferguson. Ohio History Connection. Columbus, OH.

———. Death certificate 36280, 1926, Sarah Haag. Ohio History Connection. Columbus, OH.

———. Death certificate 9146, 1938, unidentified White man. Ohio History Connection. Columbus, OH.

R.C. Hellrigle & Co.'s Columbus Directory, for 1877. Columbus, OH: R.C. Hellrigle & Co., 1877.

The Story of Columbus Past, Present and Future of the Metropolis of Central Ohio. Columbus, OH: Johnston Publishing Company, 1898.

Taylor, William Alexander. *Centennial History of Columbus and Franklin County, Ohio.* Chicago: S.J. Clarke Publishing Co., 1909.

Williams' Columbus City Directory for 1884–85. Columbus, OH: Williams and Company, 1884.

ABOUT THE AUTHOR

L ifelong Franklin County resident Nellie Kampmann works professionally in the field of history. Her love of the subject has led her to volunteer with several Columbus history and historical preservation organizations, and she was a guest historian on *The Dead Files*. At her day job, her specialty is dealing with death records. While her coworkers have nicknamed her the "Mistress of Death," she is more of an aging hippie with a gardening addiction. Her previous book, *A Haunted History of Columbus, Ohio*, reflects her interest in all things spooky.

Visit us at
www.historypress.com